# M*y*
# *Visions*
## ALONG THE
# *Poudre*
# *Valley*

*Phil Walker*

## BY

# PHIL WALKER

*Modern Visions Along the Poudre Valley*

ISBN 1-887982-13-2

Copyright ©, Walker Communications

Produced by Walker Communications, Fort Collins, CO
Printed in the United States of America by Mountain West Printing Ltd.

Published by
Walker Communications
To order books, audiocassettes, or videos contact:
Walker Communications
4134 Harbor Walk Dr.
Fort Collins, CO 80525

# Dedicated To

The People of Fort Collins.
For all you have been, and for all You are yet to become.

# Acknoweldgements

*Modern Visions Along the Poudre Valley* is a presentation to Fort Collins
through the community citizenship and gracious support of:

*First National Bank, Tom Gleason, Chairman*
*The Everitt Companies, Bob Everitt, Chairman*
*The W.W. Reynolds Companies, Bill Reynolds, President*
*Stryker-Short Foundation, Tommy and Pat Short*
*Wheeler Commercial Properties, Bill Neal, President*
*The Sitzman-Mitchell Company, Gene Mitchell, Chairman*
*The Charco-Broiler, Gib and Lynn McGarvey*
*Coldwell Banker Everitt & Williams Real Estate*

# Photographic Support

*The cover of the book is by Paul Nielsen, who has been flying
and photographing Fort Collins for over 20 years.*

*On the back cover is the author, relaxing in Old Town Square. The picture was
taken on his birthday, by his wife, Lydia Dody, Publisher of Style Magazine.*

*Lydia Dody*
*Style Magazine*
*John and Lolly Clarke*
*Kelly Ohlson*
*Northern Colorado Water Conservancy District*
*Tom and Jean Sutherland*
*Spencer Moorman*
*Gene Mitchell*
*Fort Collins Coloradoan*
*Wayne Sundberg*
*Colorado State University*
*City of Fort Collins*
*Fort Collins Public Library*

# Table of Contents _____

# *Introduction*

In the first 80 years of the life of Fort Collins, between 1873 and 1950, the population of the city increased from 20 to 15,000. In the 50 years between 1950 and 2000, the population increased from 15,000 to 112,000. I think its safe to say that the last half-century has experienced the greatest changes.

In the first Visions book, I raced through hundreds of years of history, hitting the high points and looking at the events and people who have shaped our times. The section that was devoted to the 1950 to the present was only about 20 pages, and 20% of that was about the Big Thompson Flood. I've never been satisfied with that.

When the opportunity finally arose, I embarked on this new work that is a much more detailed look at the modern era of Fort Collins. It was an eye-opener, and no doubt about it. I'm sure that most of the early settlers to the Poudre Valley could not have imagined how the city would turn out. I can't imagine it, and I lived through it.

In this book, I take us through each of the five decades since the modern times started. There was a definite beginning to this modern cycle, and there were specific reasons, nationally and locally, why Fort Collins took off and never looked back. It began with the end of World War II, and was in high gear by 1950.

Each decade possesses its own singularity, but also is part of a moving picture that has outcomes built upon previous events and attitudes. There is a real pattern to the story of Fort Collins that is not always obvious when you are living day by day. I found out that some perceptions I had of my own hometown were not entirely true.

I think you are going to learn the same thing, whether you have been in town for fifty years, fifty months, or fifty days. One question I always ask people I meet is, "How can you expect to plan a pathway to the future, if you don't have a particle of an idea how we got here from the past?" That is what this book is all about. It's the story of the events, people, ideas, opinions, and outcomes of a continuously growing population over fifty years.

The material in this book came from a stack of information, three feet high, that I have accumulated in my life in Fort Collins. Additionally, I personally interviewed over three dozen of the actual people who played a part in the development of our community. To each of them, I thank them for their time and sharing their part in our story.

Many of them shared their photographs with me, and now with you. In this effort, I have to especially thank my friend John Clarke for all he did. It was more than just the many pictures and long interviews. He also was a convenient whipping boy that I used to take out my frustrations while the labor of writing was underway. He bore the abuse with charm and good-humor.

The book was edited by Lydia Dody. Having your own wife edit your work is a unique experience. But the truth is that she is the best editor I've ever seen, and I made all her corrections without a moment's hesitation. Well, almost all of them. Here and there were some phrases or particular ways in which I said something of which I was especially proud. I probably should have taken her advise, but at least we will all know that what remains is uniquely me.

Thanks also to the individuals and companies who helped to publish the book without once asking to see a word I wrote before it was published. Of course, I didn't tell everything. Inevitably, there were many events that occurred, and many people who certainly played a part, in the story of Fort Collins in the modern era. Time and space made me leave those tales for another time and another book. At least the story of the last fifty years is a hundred times longer than it was in the first book.

I hope you enjoy it, and I hope you take away a new appreciation of how we came to be what we are as a city today.

*Phil Walker*
October, 2000

*Poudre Falls by John Clarke*

W hen something has laid quiet for some time, be it a man, or animal, or plant, when it comes to full consciousness, there is a
stirring in the heart of the entity to rise and realize its full
potential. When it is a city, there is a combination of many energies suddenly coming alive and knowing that there is a path to be followed, a dream to
realize, a future to summon. So it was for the City of Fort Collins. The
awakening of the community was like an explosion. The reverberations of
that blast have echoed through the decades and have given meaning to what
we call "The Choice City."

## The 1950s At A Glance

**1950**   • The population of Fort Collins is 14,937. Larimer County is 43,554.

**1951**   • The first water flows into Horsetooth Reservoir.

**1952**   • The trolleys are retired from Fort Collins on November 4th.

**1953**   • The Front Range is in the midst of a drought. It lasted from 1950 until 1956.

**1954**   • Dust Bowl conditions prevail in northern Colorado. Farmers have to irrigate their sugar beet seeds for germination in March. In June, temperatures reach over 100° for eight straight days. On August 6th it rains 6 inches and produces a devastating flood.

• Fort Collins telephones are switched to dials. The first exchange in town is Hunter 2, (482).

• Fort Collins votes to change its form of government from the Commissioner system to the Council-City Manager structure. Voters adopt a new City charter. Five city councilmen are installed. One of them is elected mayor.

• South College Heights subdivision is begun.

**1955**   • Cloverleaf Dog Track opens west of Loveland.

**1956**   • Fall enrollment at Colorado A&M is 4,996.

**1957**   • Colorado A&M college becomes Colorado State University.

• New Larimer County Courthouse is dedicated.

**1958**   • Fort Collins city area doubles in size in ten years to 6 squaremiles.

**1959**   • University Acres subdivision is begun. Nearly 1,000 building permits are issued during the year. T.P. Treadwell, Chief Building Inspector, wonders where all the people are coming from.

# A Front Range Treasure

Dawn was breaking over the Poudre Valley. A bright, freshly washed, clear, blue sky gleamed in the morning sun. The air was clean and fresh. It was late summer, and the day promised to be hot with late afternoon clouds piling up over the mountains, appearing magically like great ships sailing over the horizon.

Nestled at the foot of the hills that marched in ever ascending ranks to become the ramparts of the Rocky Mountains, there sat a little town. It was less than three square miles, and, within its borders, lived barely three thousand families. The wide, carefully laid out streets, formed a grid that was easy to see.

Running north and south through the middle of the town was an even wider street. There was a median through the middle of the street, and you could see one or two trolleys, at widely spaced distances, along the length of the big boulevard that the people called College Avenue.

On the north end of the big street was the commercial, downtown district. The center of downtown was marked by the intersection of College and another wide street called Mountain Avenue with a median and tracks for the trolleys running east and west.

Beginning just a short block to the northeast of this intersection there began a series of streets that ran at 45-degree angles from the two main

*FORT COLLINS, 1950. Small and compact, Fort Collins was less than 3 square miles, and had a population under 15,000 people. The city limits had not changed in 50 years. This was the last time this could be said. (Courtesy Fort Collins Public Library.)*

8

streets. This area was known as Old Town. Originally, these streets had been laid out oriented to the river, which cut on a diagonal running northwest to southeast. When the main town had been platted in 1873, all the streets were laid out on straight compass headings. But the original streets of Old Town remained, and now formed a triangle enclosed within the central scheme.

Just a few blocks north of downtown was the river. It was called the Cache la Poudre, a French term given to it by early trappers which meant, "the hiding place of the powder." The Poudre River was the reason why the town had been established in the first place. The arid West did not treat settlers kindly without a permanent water supply.

In fact, the little town looked like an oasis in the midst of a vast, treeless prairie. Along the wide streets and in the lots of the homes were many trees that had grown large and stately over the last three-quarters of a century. The neat and tidy homes, big and small, gave a good indication of the solid nature of their inhabitants.

CITY GRID. Franklin Avery drew the 1873 plat of Fort Collins. The wide streets and the regularity of the street patterns made getting around easy. (Courtesy of John Clarke)

In all ways, the town was modest and unassuming. The fifteen thousand residents, had no way of knowing that their city, floating like a jewel on the Colorado prairie, was about to be discovered by a suburban crazy public. The name, Fort Collins, was about to be talked about around the dinner tables of America, and soon, tens of thousands of families would be packing their bags and heading West just as others had done four generations before.

In August 1945, World War II finally ended.  An entire generation of Americans had gone to war and experienced the hardships of battle. Many of them had also been witnesses to the Great Depression that had ravaged America in the 1930s.  From their point of view, life owed them a break.  They were interested in a much better lifestyle than the squalor of the big cities and the never ending tedium of tenement living.  They wanted prosperity, cars, and their own homes on a real lot with real flowers to nurture and real grass to cut.

They began to spread out into the countryside of America, first on the margins of the large cities, and then to small towns that were now within reasonable distance of the bigger employment centers because of the emancipation given them by the automobile.

They had a veritable laundry list of requirements for a better life. Their new homes had to be in places with no major crime, the job market had to be plentiful, entrepreneurial vistas were a must, the climate had to be agreeable, the schools competent, nearby recreational opportunities available, higher education had to be within easy reach, and the whole package had to be affordable.  Other than that, anywhere was fine, as long as it was away from the dirty, congested cities.

The list of places that fit all these requirements was not really that long.  Soon, the very best people of America were looking at a map of Colorado and that little settlement 60 miles north of Denver.

HORSETOOTH MOUNTAIN. *The most recognizable symbol of Fort Collins. It dominates the skyline in the foothills to the west of the city. It is now a protected natural area. (Courtesy of John Clarke)*

# Quiet, But Not Asleep

In the post war period, Fort Collins had a lot of potential lying just under the surface. The people of the city had been building this potential for many years.

Their original goal was to provide opportunities for themselves and to overcome some of the limitations that had plagued them during the past twenty years.

Three principal factors gave Fort Collins the shot in the arm it needed to fuel its growth and take advantage of the improving economic time. They were expansion of our water supply, the growth of the university, and an aggressive city government that encouraged new construction and burying utilities underground.

The biggest obstacles to creating a better life in Fort Collins were the chronic shortage of water, and the lack of substantial industry and commerce to serve as a supplement to agriculture, the engine that had always been the backbone of northern Colorado. However, it was a fickle master. When there was plenty of rainfall, the price of crops came down. When top dollar was being paid for crops Larimer County farmers and ranchers could grow, the Poudre River went dry. It was a frustrating and maddening cycle of boom and bust.

Because of this unpredictability, the people of northern Colorado banded together in 1938 to propose and build the Colorado-Big Thompson Trans-Mountain Water Diversion Project...Big T, as it was known. With the help of the Colorado State legislature and the financial backing of the federal government, $168 million was allocated to build this mammoth project.

Another important component in Fort Collins was the presence of the Colorado Agriculture and Mechanical College. With the end of World War II, millions of veterans headed back to school under the benefits of the GI Bill. The college, already the biggest single employer in Fort Collins, enjoyed a major expansion because of these eager students.

In addition, the people of Fort Collins had hired an aggressive and future-thinking City administration. It was led by the very able City Manager, Guy Palmes, and supported by a progressive city council. The people and the city government were of the same mind. Everyone was interested in attracting large, stable employers who would provide jobs and an increased tax base to support the projects of civic improvements that had been held on the drawing boards waiting for the money to pay for them.

These three factors, along with the advantage of Fort Collins' favorable climate, adjacency to recreational opportunities, and the general trend in America to move West out of the stifling cities of the East, made it possible for Fort Collins to be very optimistic and upbeat about their future

# Water - Liquid Gold

Colorado is a semi-arid region with less than 15 inches of water annually. Indeed, the earliest expeditions to Colorado had all emphasized the dry nature of the region and warned that no viable agricultural industry could develop. In his 1820 exploration of Colorado, Major Stephen Long had called this area "The Great American Desert." He even wrote it on all his maps. That single statement impeded progress and immigration to the region for the next 30 years. In fact, it wasn't until gold was discovered in Colorado that pioneers began to take another look at the Front Range and start devising ways to overcome the parched nature of this land.

An entirely new approach for dealing with water rights was needed. The eastern United States didn't have a water problem. Their system of Riparian rights held that whomever owned the land bordering streams were entitled to the beneficial use of that water. It prohibited any use of water that would alter or diminish a river's flow.

POUDRE RIVER FALLS. *The river was the reason why civilization could flourish on the plains of the semi-arid Front Range. 40% of Fort Collins' drinking water is still supplied by the Cache la Poudre.* (Courtesy of John Clarke)

That concept wasn't going to work out here on the semi-arid western plains. So the Doctrine of Prior Appropriation was developed. It was based on the "first in time, first in right" principle. What this meant was that farmers could divert water from rivers or streams without regard to whoever owned the land next to the water. If the water user could show that he was putting the water to beneficial use, he could divert it according to the date on his water decree. This made water a property right that could be bought or sold.

The two principal water supplies of northern Colorado are the Poudre River and the Big Thompson River. The Poudre River originates at Poudre Lake near the top of Trail Ridge Road in Rocky Mountain National Park. It is the largest tributary of the South Platte River and supplies nearly 30% of its total flow. Annually, the 150 mile long river has an average flow of about 337,000 acre feet of water. An acre-foot of water refers to enough water to cover an acre of land one-foot deep. It's also the amount of water that an average family of four consumes in a year's time. The Poudre ends east of Greeley where it joins the South Platte.

The Big Thompson River averages 131,000 acre feet annually. It flows down the Big Thompson canyon from Estes Park, through Loveland and the southern end of the county before joining the South Platte southwest of Greeley. By the end of the 1920s, nearly all of that water was claimed, and a drought meant that some farmers would lose their crops because they couldn't get water onto their land.

During the depression years, the farmers of northern Colorado and civic leaders reopened an old subject regarding the increase in their water supply. It had been talked about since as early as 1890, but the terrible economic times, combined with the years of the dust bowls in the early 1930s made the need critical. If the valuable agricultural economy was to survive, a new source of water had to be found.

By 1933, the colossus of the Great Depression and the western dust bowl had brought Fort Collins, indeed, all of northern Colorado to its knees. In the embattled homes and offices of the city, the lights burned around the clock as the dust storms marched across the plains, endlessly, and blotted out the sun. There was no money, no jobs, no crops, no credit, and no end in sight.

The Front Range of Colorado was now paying the price for a century of exploitation. The native grasses of the plains had all been turned under for agricultural crops. Even the marginal lands had been plowed in the mad rush to get as many acres as possible under cultivation using irrigation to fuel the growth of the crops.

But now there was drought. Almost no rain had fallen for two years. The soil lay naked and exposed. The dry air sucked every drop of moisture out of the earth and left thick, choking dust behind, to blow miles high in the winds that scoured the land for two thousand miles.

Northern Colorado in 1938 had about the same population as the City of Fort Collins does today, a little over 100,000 people, mostly in the towns of Fort Collins, Loveland, Greeley, Longmont, Boulder, and Sterling. These people approached their problem at its most fundamental level. The problem was water; not enough of it to begin with, the seasonal nature of its availability, and the possibility of drought. The solution was simple. Go to the mountains, with three times the water supply as the Front Range, and divert the water from flowing west, to flow east.

Originally, Big T was called the Grand Lake Project. It was the head-water of the Colorado River, which would be the place from which the water would come.

From 1934 until 1938, the Larimer and Weld County commissioners, along with the Greeley Chamber of Commerce worked as the Northern Colorado Water Users Association. Charles Lory, President of Colorado Agricultural College in Fort Collins was able to secure a WPA grant from the federal government to develop an economic feasibility study for the project.

In 1937, the Northern Colorado Water Conservancy District was formed as an organization with proper legal standing to contract for the construction of a new water project. In 1938, the taxpayers of the district, which included seven counties of northern Colorado, all the way to the Nebraska border, overwhelmingly approved a contract with the Federal Government to build the huge project.

Construction was begun in 1938. The first part of the project was to construct the collection points near the headwaters of the Colorado River on the western side of the Continental Divide. Lake Granby and Shadow Mountain Reservoir were the principal sites to divert water from the river. To get the water to the other side of the mountains, it had to be pumped uphill and through solid rock. The 13-mile long Alva Adams tunnel was dug to accomplish that purpose.

THE ALVA ADAMS TUNNEL. *Large enough to drive a jeep through it, it was dug by hand during the late 1940s. The 13-mile long tunnel brings water from the Western Slope to the Front Range. (Courtesy of Northern Colorado Water District)*

The tunnel was dug from both ends with plans to meet in the middle. Critics of this process argued that it was madness to dig from two directions and eventually join in the center. They thought the two tunnels would just miss each other and go wandering off aimlessly and never join. In fact, the two tunnels did meet, and the error in digging calculations over the 13-mile length, was less than the width of a dime.

Even in 1938, when the economic survival of northern Colorado was at stake and there were no jobs and no water, Big T faced stiff opposition from environmentalists. The Adams tunnel had to be dug right through Rocky Mountain National Park, and opponents predicted dire ecological disaster if such construction was undertaken. They might have succeeded in blocking the project completely had it not been for the fact that when Rocky Mountain National Park was established in 1915, a provision for a future water diversion project was provided for in the charter.

The two major receptacle reservoirs for water at the eastern end of the Colorado-Big Thompson (C-BT) system were Horsetooth Reservoir and Carter Lake. Horsetooth Reservoir construction began in 1946 and was

*BUILDING SPRING CREEK DAM. Work on one of the three east-facing dams of Horsetooth Reservoir was done between 1946-49. (Courtesy Fort Collins Public Library)*

completed in 1949. The first water flowed into the reservoir in 1951. Carter Lake construction began in 1950 and was completed in 1952. Water came to that lake in 1954. Horsetooth Reservoir stores 156,000 acre feet of water, and Carter Lake holds 112,000 acre feet.

Since the 1950s, other lakes and reservoirs have come on line for the system. They include Boulder, Pinewood, and Flatiron Reservoirs. Today more than 200,000 acre feet of water flow annually from the wet Western Slope to the semi-arid farms, ranches, and towns of Eastern Colorado. Fort Collins gets about 60% of its water from C-BT, and the rest comes from the Poudre River.

Who owns all this water? About 70% of the water is used for irrigation of crops. The North Poudre Irrigation Company is the largest allottee with 13% of the water. The next biggest allottees are the cities of Fort Collins, Greeley, Loveland, Longmont, and Boulder. Together they own

*HORSETOOTH RESERVOIR. Completed in 1951, the reservoir is 7 miles long and holds over 155,000 acre-feet of water. It is a popular recreational area. (Courtesy John Clarke)*

about 27% of the water. Altogether, 30 municipalities, 120 ditch and irrigation companies, and 2,500 individuals own shares of C-BT.

Almost immediately, the system was put to the test. From 1950 through 1956, a severe drought struck the Front Range. In many places, it was worse than the dust bowl years of the 1930s. Luckily, C-BT water was the difference between having water for the crops and economic disaster.

Since 1982, Colorado has enjoyed the second longest period of wet weather in the state's history. But the records of the past have shown that dry times follow wet, and it is inevitable that drought conditions, short or prolonged, are due to arrive sometime in the Poudre Valley.

# An Educational Colossus

Who would have believed in 1870, when the Colorado Territorial Legislature designated Fort Collins as the site for the State Agricultural College, that it would turn out to be a great state University with nearly 25,000 students, and the city's biggest employer with over 8,700 employees?

CSU has come a long way from its humble beginnings. It was all very strange. In the first place, there was no state of Colorado. That didn't happen until 1876. Yet, the territorial legislature said they were going to have a state college. In the second place, there was no Fort Collins to put the college in. That didn't happen until 1873. Yet, the founders of Fort Collins insisted that there would be a city here and demanded that they get the college instead of upstart Greeley. Somehow, they got the approval and Fort Collins got the college.

However getting approval didn't mean that classes started right away.

16

*THE ORIGINAL CAMPUS. One building. Old Main built in 1878-79. It was the first building to serve as administration, and classroom for the state agricultural college. (Courtesy Fort Collins Public Library)*

It was not until 1878 that the city got around to building the first formal classroom building. This structure, known as Old Main, was the signal that Fort Collins was serious about having a college.

On September 1, 1879, Elijah Edwards, the college's president, and two teachers welcomed the first students to enroll for classes. Five students showed up. Two of them were the president's children. By the end of the first semester, 20 students were enrolled. The first graduating class was three people in June of 1884.

By the turn of the century, a huge battle for the identity of the college was raging. The Colorado Cattle and Horse Growers Association wanted to keep the school an Ag college. Others wanted a broader curriculum. The supporters of Liberal Arts won out, but not before several faculty members and the college president, Barton Aylesworth, were fired.

In 1909, Charles Lory, after whom the Lory Student Center was named, became president. He served for 31 years, which was longer than any other person had. Under his leadership, the enrollment of the college increased from 217 to 2,048 students. Lory was forced out in 1940 because of criticism that he had spent more time working on the Colorado-Big Thompson water project than running the school.

Lory's replacement was Roy Green. He came at

*LONGTIME CSU PRESIDENT. Charles Lory was president of the college for 31 years, from 1909 till 1940. The Lory Student Center is named in his honor. (Courtesy Colorado State University)*

a bad time.  World War II had begun and enrollment tumbled.  During the war years enrollment went down to just 701 students and there was some doubt whether the college could survive at all.  Green had plans to

THE 1950 CAMPUS.  Nearly all the campus was located around The Oval.  By 1950, enrollment at the college had grown to nearly 4,000 students, many of whom were GI Veterans.  (Courtesy Fort Collins Public Library)

greatly expand the college to handle the influx of servicemen that were sure to show up, but he never got to implement them.  In 1946, while dining at the Brown Palace Hotel in Denver, a deranged ex-serviceman shot him.  He survived the shooting, but never recovered his health and died two years later.

At the end of World War II, enrollment in the college soared.  During the 1946-47 academic year, 3,518 students attended the school, which, by then, had been renamed Colorado Agricultural and Mechanical School.  Of that total, 2,517 were veterans.  The men had come from overseas and were eager to get a better education and to take advantage of the GI Bill offered by the federal government to help pay for their tuition.

A PROGRESSIVE PRESIDENT. Dr. William E. Morgan was the 9th president for the college.  Under his leadership, the college became Colorado State University and enrollment increased over threefold.  Shown here on the left with Fort Collins Mayor Harvey Johnson.  (Courtesy Fort Collins Public Library)

In 1949, a far-sighted man became president of the college.  This was William Morgan.  He was the school's eighth president and would serve for 20 years.  It was his vision that propelled the college into modern times.  Morgan understood that the post war era would bring millions of new students to university campuses all over the country. He knew that the college was going to have to emerge as a progressive educational institution. He foresaw the need for major campus expansions and enthusiastically lobbied the state legislature to get them. Most of the current residence halls were built during his administration. He expanded the curriculum in all areas and vastly increased library acquisitions.

In 1955, the college awarded its first doctoral degree. Interestingly, this degree was given to A.R. Chamberlain, who would later succeed Morgan as president of the university.

In May 1957, Colorado A&M college became Colorado State University. This was a reflection of the expansion of sponsored research and graduate programs. International studies gave legitimacy to the title of "university."

All this growth in both students and facility provided jobs and a higher level of economic activity for Fort Collins. The university itself became an industry, and it was the best kind. It was clean, non-polluting, and high tech. The employment it provided was base jobs with large paychecks. This meant that steady capital was flowing into the community marketplace. The entire service industry of Fort Collins benefited. The retailers of food, clothing, furniture, appliances, housing, entertainment and so on expanded to take advantage of the demand. This produced more jobs and more opportunity. The result was an upturn in the local economy. With more purchasing by consumers going on, more revenues were being produced in sales and use taxes and the city government was able to start planning for real capital improvements in roads, parks, utilities and other basic city services. The city was quick to take advantage of this windfall.

# City Government. Quick On the Trigger

By the end of 1945, America had been through 15 very difficult years. First, The Great Depression brought the country to its knees economically. In the West, conditions were compounded by a severe drought that created the time of Dust Bowls. On the eve of the United States entry into the war, Fort Collins had a population of about 9,000 people, and nearly 20% of the homes in town were empty. It was just miserable.

Then came Pearl Harbor and the boys of Larimer County marched off to fill the ranks of the military. The economy, spurred by massive government spending, began to improve somewhat, but now there was the gnawing fear that a son or a husband or brother would be killed fighting somewhere in the world in a place the family could not even pronounce.

THE BOYS COME HOME. *Triumphant soldiers return home from World War II. They were looking for a better life, better housing, better jobs. Many of them would find what they wanted in Fort Collins (Courtesy US Army)*

So, with the end of the war everyone was ready for a little peace and prosperity. The GI's, all 13 million of them, began to stream home at the rate of a million a month. They found there was no place for them to live. They moved in with their parents, doubled up in crowded apartments, and even used unoccupied military barracks.

In 1947, a man named William Levitt hit upon the notion of building houses like they built cars, on an assembly line. Levitt bought 6,000 acres in Nassau County, New York and started putting up houses at a breakneck speed. In 4 years, he built 17,447 homes.

These home were not very glamorous. There were only about a half dozen floor plans. They were boxy and not very big. But that didn't matter a bit to the thousands of couples who camped out for days for a chance to buy one. 82,000 moved in. Young couples now had the opportunity to blossom, to have the security and the comfort of their own homes, to have a little patch of grass, and a place to raise their family. A robust economy, the GI bill, and federally subsidized mortgages aided them in this.

In the 1950s, 13 million new homes were built in the United States. 11 million of them were in the new areas on the outskirts of the cities. The term "suburbia" became a part of the English language.

The boom was not long in arriving in Fort Collins. It was not a wholesale, mass-produced build up such as Levittown; the emerging class of developers in town were a good deal more conservative. Still, the need was there and the City of Fort Collins wanted to do everything it could to encourage it.

Howard Evans, City Engineer for the City of Fort Collins was concerned. There was just nothing going on in his town. Nobody was building anything. The year was 1951, and Evans could see Americans pouring out of the cities and migrating to the Sunbelt states and to the Golden West, by the millions. He wanted some of that growth for our town.

Just then, fate stepped in, carefully disguised as Alvin Miller, slightly out of breath.

"Howard," said Alvin, "there's some empty land across the street from my house on City Park Avenue. I want to buy the land, divide it up into lots, and sell it to some local contractors to build houses on.

What's it going to cost me to put in streets, curbs, gutters, sewer and water?"

Evans thought for a moment and then said, "Nothing."

"I beg your pardon?"

"I'm not going to charge you anything right now," said Evans. "You just go ahead and give me a plan about how you want to divide this land up, and then pay us back for the city improvements as you sell off the lots."

*SPREADING OUT. The first of the new subdivisions, built beginning in 1951 by Alvin Miller, in west Fort Collins. The homes sold for a little over $10,000. (Courtesy of John Clarke)*

"That's a pretty sweet deal, Howard," said Alvin. "Why are you doing it?

"Because we need some more houses in this town. When people find out what a good town Fort Collins actually is, they will want to move here. This way they will have something to move into."

That's just what they did. Miller divided the land, located between Shields and City Park Avenue into 20 lots. In short order, he had sold every one of them. It was the first new construction in Fort Collins in a decade. Miller paid back the city for the improvements and started looking for a new project.

He soon found it. To the west of City Park Avenue and south of Mulberry, was another parcel of land that Miller could buy. He sketched out an extension of Sheldon Drive from City Park and created a new street he called Westview. Along the new streets he platted in 12 lots. Evans was helpful in the planning, but didn't offer to front the street improvements this time. In fact, he never offered to do such a thing like that again.

This second set of Miller lots, in 1954, included the first of the many homes that he would build over the next 15 years. The homes were built specifically for GI's. They were 3 bedroom, 900 square foot homes with one bath homes and a carport. The homes sold for $10,500. The payments on them, including principal, interest, taxes and insurance were $115 a month. The interest rate was 4%. They didn't last very long.

In those days, the city approval process was simple. Howard Evans was the engineer and planning and zoning board all rolled into one man. You walked into his office, showed him what you wanted to do, paid a $40 fee, and a few weeks later you got your building permit. The developers have always paid the costs of street improvements, curbs, gutters, and utilities.

After 1954, Miller and a growing number of others developed quite a few lots. In practice you would buy the land, go through the approval process, sometimes no more than sketching out your ideas on a napkin at the coffee shop, although Miller said that the process was often not that formal, and then put in all the improvements. When the streets, sidewalks, and the rest of the improvements were finished, Miller would sell his lots to many small contracting companies. The price, including the improvements, was about $2,000 to $2,500. The density was generally 3 lots per acre.

People in Fort Collins today have a hard time imagining what Fort Collins looked like in the 1950s. The simplest way to put it is that Fort Collins wasn't. The town was still very tiny. When we talk about building homes around the City Park, south of Mulberry, we aren't talking about infill. All the land was empty of homes. It was mostly small farms that spread out, for as far as you could see, all the way to the foothills.

When Alvin Miller moved across the Mercer Ditch to build homes in the vacant land that spread out all the way to Taft Hill Road, it was a big deal. People remarked that Fort Collins was finally moving out. Miller had to build a bridge across the ditch. He asked the city engineer what he wanted and he told him. Then he built it, simple as that. One stipulation that the city made was that they wanted a chain link fence put up to keep kids from falling into the ditch. Miller asked how far he had to get back from the ditch to get out of the Ditch Company's right of way and nobody had the faintest idea. He went pouring through the old records and found out that the right of way from the bank had to be wide enough for a team of horses and a slip. So he got out his tape and measured two horses, and then put in his fence. Nobody ever said a word about that. The bridge and the chain link fence remain as they were built, even today.

One of the popular conceptions is that home development was done on huge blocks of land. That turns out not to be the case, at least as far as Alvin Miller was concerned. The largest plot of land he ever bought to develop was only 40 acres. Still, between 1957 and 1973, he developed over a thousand lots and homes.

*A BIG, MODERN SUBDIVISION was begun in 1954 by Mae Tiley and her son Bill, and was called South College Heights. It featured curved streets and cul-de-sacs for family safety. (Courtesy of John Clarke)*

Another developer was also busy in Fort Collins beginning in the 1950s. This was Bill Tiley and his project was the very visible South College Heights. The subdivision began south of Spring Creek, along College Avenue, all the way to Drake Road. Once again, all this land was completely vacant. It was another farm on the edge of town. Tiley used more of the Levittown concepts with his development. He built a lot of houses, with a limited numbers of floor plans. He developed the subdivision in just a few short years. The homes were modest in size, but perfectly acceptable for the buying public who hungered for the chance to own their own home.

LITTLE BOOMERS. In the 1950s, the Baby Boom explosion was in full swing. Families were growing and Fort Collins was an ideal place to raise the children. (Courtesy of John Clarke)

Using some of the most commonly accepted modern practices of subdivision design; South College Heights featured curved streets, lots of cul-de-sacs, and no alleys. This fit the style of the times. America was going through a baby boom, so there were lots of little kids. Curved streets slowed down the traffic. Cul-de-sacs were safer places for kids to play since the traffic did not go through. It was just perfect for young families

There were, as it turned out, significant problems with the whole concept. The streets did not lend themselves to traffic movement. There were no real feeder streets and certainly no arterials in the entire subdivision. It was kind of like a giant maze. You went in and just kept driving around and around. This was very tedious for people in their cars.

A worse problem, however, was the way the subdivision was placed to begin with. Up until South College Heights was built, Prospect Street was the city limits. It was also the end of the platting plan of the city drawn by Franklin Avery back in 1873. This meant that the big 100 foot wide streets ended at Prospect. The city should have insisted that at least one of these streets between College and Lemay be used as an arterial. But none of them were. The entire area between Prospect and the boundary of South College Heights turned out to be a hodgepodge of conflicting streets that provided no through traffic. In order for traffic to move north and south along the main axis of the town, they had to use College Avenue or go all the way over to Lemay, a mile away. This put a lot of early pressure on College Avenue as a main thoroughfare, and produced a traffic problem way before the actual number of cars in Fort Collins justified it.

The problem was only compounded as the years went by with the addition of the Landings subdivision. By the time the Landings were being developed, the city knew full well that they had an access problem, but they approved the design of the subdivision anyway. It was justified because Warren Lake was a geographical impediment and building a road around it was difficult.

# City Government Changes

Near the middle of the 1950s, Fort Collins was really rolling along. Horsetooth Reservoir was filling up, albeit slowly since Colorado was in the middle of a drought. The College was expanding at breakneck speed, from a low of 701 students during World War II, to 4,000 students by the middle of the decade. The city administration was encouraging development by making it easier for builders to construct homes. Alvin Miller was building steadily in the west part of town, and Mae and Bill Tiley had begun their large subdivision of South College Heights. The population of the town was approaching 20,000.

The city government thought it was time to ask the people again to modernize city government. Back in 1938, the city had tried to get the voters to approve a change from the old commissioner form of government and had been flatly refused. This was a big surprise to the city officials who just couldn't understand why the people objected. After all, they had laid out their case very elegantly to the people, "Ladies and Gentlemen, it is time for Fort Collins to progress in a modern society and adopt the form of government that is used by almost every city of any size in the country. We have used the outdated and very inefficient

"City Commissioner" form of government since 1913!"

"A City Manager form of government lets us hire a trained professional whose job it will be to hire a staff, run the city services including fire, police, streets, parks, and courts, all under the direction and control of an elected body of citizens who sit on the city council. It will be more efficient, cheaper and more responsive to your needs as citizens."

How did something so reasonable and so natural to adopt, go down to such ignominious defeat? Well, the reason is because the government system of Commissioners in Fort Collins actually worked. It worked very well indeed, and the people felt more than justified about being somewhat cautious in dumping their neat old commissioners system to some high-handed professional from the outside, who they didn't know from Adam. The people just said, "no thanks."

That is the way it was. Commission government worked sort of like a Presidential Cabinet. Each person, or commissioner, was responsible for some element of the government. So, we had a commissioner of finance, utilities, streets, parks, and so forth. The idea was to allow for the specialization of talent. A person did what he or she was good at instead of having to be all things to all people.

Well, the commissioner form of government was made just for Fort Collins. The city had a lot of people who could specialize in the various governmental departments. Since they never did pay the commissioners any real salaries, the people had to serve on a voluntary basis, since most of them had businesses to run or jobs as well.

The weakness to the commissioner form of city government was that it was so easily corrupted. Fortunately, in the case of Fort Collins, the people who ran for commissioner were not only talented, but also honest...as pure as the driven snow. The system worked here because a team of conscientious, honest and hard working men and women ran it. There never was any corruption, graft, kickbacks, dishonesty, crime, or any of the other horrors of the modern city, as far as anyone knows.

At any rate, when the city government, meaning these very same overworked commissioners, went to the voters to change to a City Council/City Manager kind of government, the voters said no in a very loud voice. That was a setback, but not for long. The commissioners of Fort Collins knew that they couldn't keep up with all the work much longer. Besides, it was ridiculous to have the commissioner of utilities, personally go over to some lady's house and unplug her plumbing, when he had a business of his own to run. So, the city commissioners did the only thing they could, under the circumstances. They hired a city manager anyway: exactly what the voters had told them they didn't want them to do.

As it turned out, there was no scandal, no special prosecutors, no outcry for recalls. There were two reasons for this. First, the idea of a city manager really was the right answer for the Fort Collins that was soon to emerge. There were only about 9,000 people in town and all of them could talk to each other in the span of a week. This new City Manager wasn't such a bad person after all. The city ran better.

The second reason the commissioners got away with their little heresy was because of the quality of the individual that the commissioners hired. His name was Guy Palmes and he was the City Manager of Fort Collins from the beginning in 1938 until 1961. He was a very able administrator, highly innovative, and well liked. In many ways, much of the character and

THE FIRST CITY MANAGER. *Guy Palmes. City Manager of Fort Collins from 1938-61. His leadership gave Fort Collins a jump-start toward building and prosperity. (Courtesy Fort Collins Public Library)*

appearance of modern Fort Collins is a result of the direction of Palmes during 23 years of administration.

Now the times had changed. Fort Collins wasn't a sleepy little village any more. It was a vibrant, growing community. The old commissioners system was totally inadequate to handle the administration of the town. It was producing planning problems (little mistakes that would have big consequences in the future), like the lack of providing for continuous north/south arterials to the east of College Avenue toward Lemay. The city was determined to do something about it. This time they went about it in the right way. They went out and lobbied for the support of the League of Women Voters, the Chamber of Commerce, and the principal service clubs in town. They made the same arguments they had in 1938, but this time they were able to show that the system was truly archaic and had to be replaced with a more efficient form of government. Besides, they already had half the system in place with a city manager that most people liked, although he had a reputation for being somewhat dictatorial.

A petition was circulated in town for the convening of a charter convention. This was truly a major undertaking. It meant that a whole new charter was about to be adopted. It would be the same thing if the United States were to pass a referendum calling for a new constitutional convention. Fort Collins was about to be reorganized from the ground up by the grass roots of its people.

The convention ran for 60 days during the summer of 1954. There were 21 delegates to the convention who had been elected by the people. Fort Collins lawyer Ralph Harden was one of the delegates.

He remembers that the principal controversy in the group was what form of government they would choose. There were those who opposed the idea of a weak city council and a strong city manager. Some advocated the idea of a strong mayor who would be the leading advocate of the peoples' business with the city manager being just an administrator. Bill Stover, also a member of the group was one of many delegates who didn't want to change the system at all. He argued that the commissioner system had been effective for decades and saw no reason to change it.

However, there were those in the city who were very suspicious of the apparently small group of people who always seemed to be the decision makers when it came time to select city leaders. They contended that it was members of the local Elks Club who got chosen to run for city leadership positions, and they always won. This group wanted more city councilmen, popularly elected.

In the end, a majority of the delegates came to believe that the city government should be run on a day by day basis by the city manager and that the city council would set the policy. They never intended the job to be a very big one, so they set the salaries of the council at little more than an honorarium. The mayor was just one member of the council and his was mostly a ceremonial position. He didn't even have an office in the city hall. This made the city manager the one who carried the biggest stick in town. Of course, if he didn't carry out the policy that the council set for him, they could always fire him and get someone who would.

This business of setting policy was set up to be extremely simple. The council was supposed to be able to sit down with the city manager and say, "After we have paid all the help, paid all the bills and set aside a little money for a prudent reserve, do we have any money left?" The city manager would then say yes or no. If he said no, they fired him, if he said yes, they said, "OK, go out and build a new park on the west side of town," or, "We want such and such street paved and widened." The city manager then did what they said.

The charter was finished in time for the November elections and submitted to the voters, who overwhelmingly approved it.

The first thing the new council, comprised of William Allen, Mayor Robert Sears, Rolland Ellis, J. Morris Howell, and Frank Aydelotte did

28

THE OLD CITY HALL. Built in 1882, the old city hall on Walnut Street downtown, was the home of the city administration, police department, and fire department. Restored in the 1980s, it is now a private residence and office building. (Courtesy of John Clarke)

was to say to the city manager, "Do we have any money left over?" He said yes, and so the council said, "Build a new city hall on Laporte Street and get us out of this rundown building that was built in 1882." And that's what they did.

City Manager Guy Palmes presided over the surge of Fort Collins in the 1950s. Just like everyone else in the country, Palmes had to make a paradigm shift in thinking to accommodate the new realities. Palmes was driven by the fact that he knew Fort Collins was going to be attractive to a lot of people. What he needed was an edge to spur growth and cash in on the flood of immigrants as they passed by.

After giving it some thought, Palmes hit upon a great idea. The whole country was littered with overhead power lines. They were unsightly, dangerous, and had to be replaced every few years. A few cities in America had taken to putting these power lines underground, but the cost of doing this was running as much as five hundred dollars a lot. In an era when a whole house cost less than $10,000, that was a heavy expense. Still, burying all the utilities had a great deal of visual appeal. They also lasted a lot longer than the overhead lines. Palmes decided that he would bite the bullet and subsidize the burying of utilities and offer the benefit to the developers of the city. He announced that the price would be just $50 per lot. Not surprisingly, the developers jumped at the incentive. New construction boomed.

Soon, people would come into Fort Collins, drive around the wide streets, smell the clean, dry air, look at the university, survey the economic opportunity, and say, "Gee, this is a nice town, let's move here." Part of the reason was what they didn't see as much as what they did. The landscape was not cluttered up with unsightly power lines. Palmes was way ahead of his time.

# Father Goose

Once upon a time, there were almost no Canadian geese in Fort Collins. The flyway, the natural migration route for the birds, was about 50 miles to the east. The sight of a flock of geese around Fort Collins was very rare.

This situation was of concern to a man named Gurney Crawford. Crawford was a conservation officer for the Colorado Department of Game and Fish. In 1951, the local game and fish office was on an 80-acre tract of land near Wellington. It was a marshy, weed infested swamp. That made it lousy for home-building, terrible for farming, and grazing cattle was out of the question. Late on fall afternoon, Gurney was viewing his little empire darkly.

FATHER GOOSE. The amazing Gurney Crawford. He was responsible for bringing the Canadian Geese back to Fort Collins and was a national conservation award winner. (Courtesy Fort Collins Public Library)

"This land ought to be good for something," he said. "The state doesn't think its worth a hoot or they wouldn't have stuck us out here, but I ought to be able to find a use for it."

Just then, a small flock of Canadian Geese came flying over.

Gurney watched them as they majestically circled his swamp and then swooped in for a landing on the marshy, wet earth. The geese fed for a while and then seemed contented to settle down for the night, all but disappearing into the high weeds. That gave Gurney an idea. He didn't see Canadian geese in these parts very often. He liked them. They were pretty. He wanted more of them.

Gurney got to studying the situation and found out that there were actually quite a few lakes and marshes and open land dotted around the Fort Collins area that would make wonderful nesting and resting areas for the geese, and for ducks too.

The trick was to change the habits of the birds. Canadian geese are creatures of habit. They have a tendency to return to the same places year after year, and the will often nest in the same spot where they were born.

So, Gurney became an egg-napper. He raided the nests of geese farther to the east and brought them back to his office to hatch. He also went all over, talking to farmers and ranchers who had lakes and ponds on their properties. He convinced them to let him set up little habitats for his birds. He built hundreds of crude box nests and sprinkled them around the Fort Collins area. He trapped birds, banded them, raised them, and then he let them go.

Sure enough, a bunch of the birds came back the following year. Gurney worked hard to keep people from shooting his birds on his protected lands, and he made a veritable paradise out of his Game and Fish grounds. More birds arrived.

Within just a few years, there were thousands of Canadian geese nesting and resting and eating and hatching more little geese in the area surrounding and actually in Fort Collins. The climate was mild compared to the Arctic north, and the food supply was plenty to serve a growing population of birds.

Over the years, Crawford single-handedly altered the natural flyway of the Canadian geese and several species of ducks, and earned the nickname, "Father Goose," In 1973, Gurney Crawford received the American Motors Conservation award for his accomplishments.

Today, there are about 60,000 Canadian geese who return to Fort Collins every year, and a permanent population of about 6,000. The city has adopted the goose as its symbol on its letterheads and city signs.

Of course, those residents who live near the lakes and waterways that are frequented by the geese are not always so happy about their presence. Still, most of the people of Fort Collins really like their geese. And the geese seem to like it here too. In fact, many a story has been told of rush hour traffic on a busy street coming to a complete halt while a mother goose and a half dozen furry little goslings mosey across the street. They seem to know that everybody is going to stop for them. Well, why not? There was a time when they were here when there wasn't even a Fort. They have just reclaimed what was always theirs, compliments of the big heart of Gurney Crawford, "Father Goose."

# Public Works for Public Institutions

The mid 1950s produced a flood of changes in public works. On all fronts the city, county, and university exploded with public projects.

*A COMPLETED BUILDING. Everyone agreed that the new City Hall was a beautiful addition to the city. (Courtesy of John Clarke)*

The City of Fort Collins, reorganized under a new city charter, began work on a new city hall. The council decided that it should be built in Washington Park. The vote was taken in March 1956. The building was placed near the corner of Laporte and Howes, and was a replacement for the old city hall on Walnut Street that had been used since 1882. One of the driving principals to building a new city hall, besides the fact that the old one was much to small to handle all the business of a growing city, was that it gave the administration the chance to build two fire stations. Up until then, the single fire station for the entire town was in the old city hall. People worried all the time about what they would do if a train were rolling through town at the same time a fire broke out on the west side of Fort Collins. That had never happened, but people worried about the possibility. The new city hall would contain the city administration, utility office with a drive through to pay your bills, and the police department. Two new fire stations were built on opposite sides of the train tracks. The cornerstone for the new city hall was laid on August 17, 1957, near the 93rd anniversary of the founding of the original Fort. Mayor Robert Sears presided over the ceremony.

The county was also busy in expanding its services. Up until 1957, there had been three Larimer County Courthouses. The first one was no more than a log cabin that had been moved from Laporte when Fort Collins became the county seat in 1868. Afterwards, the Old Grout building at the corner of Linden and Jefferson served as the courthouse. Finally, in 1887, the grand old two story, Victorian courthouse with its big clock tower was built on the square bounded by Mason, Mountain, Howes and Oak Streets.

*THE 1887 LARIMER COUNTY COURTHOUSE. A stately Victorian building that housed the county services. A near replica of the courthouse is today the Disneyland City Hall on Main Street at the Disney Parks. (Courtesy Fort Collins Public Library)*

The courthouse was constructed of fine red brick at a cost of $39,370. It was more than just a courthouse. It also served as offices for the county treasurer, clerk and recorder, and assessor. The county jail was located in the basement of the building.

There were two entrances to the building on opposite sides. If a person had business on the second floor of the building, you could come down the stairs and go out either way. It didn't take convicted felons long to figure out that one deputy could not go in two directions at once, so the first time two felons left the district court from the second floor, under the guard of one sheriff's officer, they split up and took off

*THE 1957 LARIMER COUNTY COURTHOUSE. Built on the same site as the 1887 courthouse, it was built with no bond money for $1.63 million. It served as the Larimer County Courthouse until the new Justice Center was completed in 2000. (Courtesy Fort Collins Public Library)*

in two directions. One was apprehended immediately, but it took a little longer to apprehend the second one.

When the old courthouse was razed in 1957, a group of gavels were carved out of the railing in one of the courts, and were presented to each member of the bar in practice at that time. Among the attorneys present who received a gavel was Ralph Harden. He would have the distinction of being about the only attorney to practice in three Larimer County Courthouses, including the old, old courthouse, the one that was constructed in the same location after it was torn down, and the brand new Justice Center, completed in 2000. Harden also purchased all the brick in the old, old courthouse and laboriously cleaned and stacked 10,000 of them to build his home.

In 1957, the fourth Larimer County Courthouse was built on the site of the 1887 building. Planning for this courthouse had begun back in 1946. The commissioners raised the mil levy rate by one mil to start setting aside money to build a new building. Over the next several years, the mil levy was raised to three mils and by 1955, the county had accumulated $1.63 million dollars. That's how much the new courthouse cost to build. The commissioners and the people were very proud of the fact that they were able to build the courthouse without a bond issue.

Dedication was on Sunday, August 11, 1957. The ceremony was presided over by District Judge Dale E. Shannon, with the mayors of the five Larimer County cities and other dignitaries looking on.

Meanwhile, the college was in the middle of a massive expansion to house and teach the growing number of students whom were pouring into the college every fall. William E. Morgan, the eighth president of the school was proceeding with a $25 million dollar expansion. Ten new dormitories were constructed, the Foothills campus was initiated, and several new classroom buildings were built.

On May 1, 1957, Colorado A&M college became Colorado State University. The Aggies became the Rams, and everybody wondered what to do with the giant "A" on the foothills west of town. Some of the newcomers thought that it should be wiped out, but the sentimental natives of Fort Collins just couldn't bring themselves to destroy the landmark that had been visible from everywhere in town for the previous 30 years. So it remains today, brightly repainted every year, a sentimental anachronism.

# Emerging and Receding Industry

The industrial base of Fort Collins was in a state of transition in the 1950s. Since the turn of the century, the city economy was rooted in agriculture. The biggest examples of this was the sugar beet industry, and the lamb feeding operations. Fort Collins first self made millionaire,

*NOT SO BAAAAD! Lamb feeding and sheep production was the biggest in America in Larimer County. It was a powerful economic factor for over 50 years. (Courtesy Fort Collins Public Library)*

*THE GREAT WESTERN SUGAR BEET PLANT. Built in 1904 at a cost of over a million dollars, the plant produced over 15 million pounds of sugar annually. Closed in 1955. (Courtesy Fort Collins Public Library)*

Benjamin Hottel had made his money by putting together a consortium which raised $1.25 million in 1903 to construct a sugar beet plant on Vine Drive, east of College Avenue.

By 1904, the sugar beet plant was processing 15 million pounds of granulated sugar a year.  By 1910, the plant had put nearly 8 million dollars into the Larimer County economy in wages and purchase of sugar beets from the farmers.  These days that doesn't sound like a lot of money, but think of it in proportion to the economy of the day.  In 1900, the average weekly wage for a man was ten dollars, a loaf of bread was a nickel, and the very same sugar sold for four cents a pound.  So, to get an idea of what money was really worth in those days you have to multiply by a factor of at least ten to one.

Nevertheless, the one-two punch of the powerful sugar beet industry and the equally muscular lamb feeding and wool growing concerns were propelling the rest of the business community.  Larimer County was feeding over 400,000 lambs annually.  This made it the number one center for this business in the entire country.  It had such a huge impact on the town, that Fort Collins High School adopted the Lambkin as a mascot, much to the chagrin of generations of future graduates.

However, by the middle of the decade in the 1950s, sugar beets and lamb feeding had seen better days.  The sugar beet industry had been reducing the acreage of sugar beets for a number of years due to a fall in demand and high prices, and was all but destroyed by the drought and high winds of that time.  In May 1955, The Great Western Sugar Company announced that it would not operate the plant that fall.  It was never reopened.

A new generation of industry was developing in Fort Collins. Foremost of these was the construction business.  New homes, offices, stores and a huge expansion of construction at CSU was producing thousands of new jobs.

Everywhere there was a vibrancy and a sense of purpose to a city that had found its stride and was doing all it could to create the most successful city possible.  After so many years of watching other towns grow up, it was time for this town to come of age and realize all the potential it could imagine.  Fort Collins was able to imagine quite a lot.

One of the early industrial enterprises was Forney Industries.  J.D. Forney was a homegrown entrepreneur who developed a portable welding machine.  It was a wonderful tool for farmers and ranchers, and Forney went all over the country peddling the welders.  Sometimes he got cash, other times he bartered.  In any case, his business flourished.

Soon, Forney Industries had established a manufacturing plant on the West Side of town on Laporte Street.  It was outside of the city limits

then, and remains so, even until today.

Forney was an independent, free thinker. His fertile mind cranked out one innovation after another. He was also civic minded. After the suspension of trolley service, he volunteered to go into the business of providing bus service for the community. It was supposed to be a break even or a little better proposition, but the system was a money loser from the very beginning. By 1955, Forney had all he wanted of a bus system and the city had a special election in December to ask the voters to take on the job. Following a successful vote, the city embarked on the public transportation business.

There was no grass growing under Forney's feet. He had what he thought was a wonderful idea. He was convinced that America was ready for personal airplanes the same way they had been ready for personal cars. He embarked on a program to mass-produce a little single-engine; two-seater plane called an Aircoupe. It was to be manufactured in Fort Collins. Only a few of the planes were ever produced and the whole company was eventually sold off to Beech Aircraft in Wichita, Kansas.

Meanwhile Forney had become some disillusioned with the troubles he had experienced with the city of Fort Collins. He withdrew from almost all public view and moved his splendid

PERSONAL AIR TRAVEL. J.D. Forney believed that people would use private airplanes the way they used private cars. He built the Aircoupe from his Fort Collins facility. (Courtesy Fort Collins Public Library)

collection of antique cars to Denver. Today, the Forney Transportation Museum with one of the largest collection of antique and classic cars in the world is in new quarters across from the Denver Coliseum.

Another company that made its first appearance in 1955 was

Woodward Governor. Initially the company was only hiring students, but within a few years had established a manufacturing plant in downtown Fort Collins.

# Of Boats and Bravado

Although Horsetooth Reservoir was built to provide a vital new water supply to northern Colorado, it didn't take the people very long to figure out that it was perfect for all sorts of recreation. Soon boats of

every description were being launched on the big reservoir for fishing, water skiing, and fun. This corresponded to the surge in boating that was sweeping an affluent America at that time. The "in thing" was to have a boat and use it on the weekends.

*WHATEVER FLOATS YOUR BOAT. Horsetooth Reservoir floated the boats of the 1950s, when boating became a popular American pastime. (Courtesy of John Clarke)*

The reservoir saw the establishment of the "Sail and Saddle Club," a private, members-only organization that provided a private dock, clubhouse, and beach. It was busy all the time. The installation of the dock meant that members could leave their boats moored all summer and not go through the hassle of hauling the boat up to the reservoir every weekend and launching it.

One of the members of the club was a successful businessman and investor named Gene Rouse. He was well liked and popular, and enjoyed a playful game of oneupsmanship with his friends. He announced one spring in the mid 1950s that he had ordered one of the new inboard boats. He bragged that his boat would be the fastest on the lake. He droned on and on about his new boat so much that a couple of his friends, Bob Busch and Gordon Walker decided to put him in his place.

The two of them went down to the train station and made a deal with the freight agent. They told him to call them when the boat arrived, before he called Rouse. He said he would, and a few days later the boat came in. The two friends went to the switching yard and found the boat on a flat bed train car. They had prepared specially printed tags that they put inside the instruction manual and attached to the motor. It said, "WARNING! Due to the high performance nature of this engine, a period of adjustment is necessary before it can be operated at high speeds. You should not operate the engine at more than 500 rpms until after it has been run for no less than 100 hours. Violation of this provision will invalidate your warranty."

Rouse came rushing down to the train station to take delivery of his boat. He dutifully read the warning label. The following weekend he launched his shiny, new inboard boat at the Sail and Saddle Club. He announced that he would have to break in the engine before he ran it at full speed, but when he had, that it would be the fastest boat on the lake.

Of course, no such requirement was necessary for this engine, and 500 rpms was barely enough to keep the boat barely awash. The fishing boats were trolling faster than Rouse was running.

All summer long Rouse laboriously chugged back and forth in front of the docks at the club. Everybody was in on the gag except him. They snickered or laughed uproariously as he lumbered along, looking ridiculous in his snappy white cap that he had bought just for the purpose.

Finally, when the boating season was close to the end, he was let in on the secret. Walker and Busch announced to Rouse, in front of the assembled membership that he had been taken in by their prank.

You never saw such an angry man in your life. He cursed and ranted. He kicked things off the dock. He stormed up and down, all to the hoots of laughter from the assembled multitude. In the end, he jumped in his boat and roared off at high speed until he was just a speck on the horizon.

In the end, he forgave his friends. Everybody wanted him to pull them on their water skis, because he really did have the fastest boat on the lake.

As a postscript to this story, Gene Rouse went on to be one of the founding directors of a new company in Fort Collins, Water-Pik.

# We Really are...Main Street

There was once a model railroad enthusiast. His name was Harper Goff. By profession, he was a graphic designer and illustrator. Among his claims to fame was the creation of the Jolly Green Giant that everyone has seen in the television commercials. Goff shared his model railroad zeal with other friends, and one day was talking with one of them.

"Harper," said the man, "I'm planning on building a new kind of amusement park. Its not going to be anything like what people are used to seeing. It will have a theme, or several themes. I want to make a statement at the entrance to the park that depicts America sometime near the turn of the century. I want to capture the spirit of the country in more serene times. Can you help me design that?"

Goff said he would work on it, and that he had just the setting in mind for such a theme. He told his friend that he had grown up in a town that had all sorts of wonderful old buildings that would certainly capture the idea.

He returned to his hometown in the early 1950s, and sure enough, all the buildings he remembered as he was growing up were still there. He took many photographs of these stately old buildings, and then returned to his studio to put the concept on paper.

Goff's friend was delighted with the drawings and encouraged him to do more of them. Before long, a whole community was created that captured the picture of America in bygone days. The friend brought the entire concept to life in his new amusement park. He called the little town, Main Street.

This is how Main Street at Disneyland in California was created. The friend was Walt Disney and his park was opened in 1955. Disney created his "mood setter" to the park depicting America sometime around the turn of the century with stately Victorian buildings, trolley cars, and park-like plazas imbedded in the urban setting.

The Carnation Company Emporium on one of the corners is a dead ringer for the old Poudre Valley Bank in Old Town at the corner of Linden and Walnut. The trolleys are not much like the Fort Collins trolleys because they are drawn along the tracks by horses, but the trolley went right through the middle of the street, just as it did in Fort Collins.

One of the real neat features of Main Street is the park at the end of the street where you can go in several directions to visit the other lands of Disneyland. It's a big circle with grass in the center of the street, which has the trolley tracks going around it. That was what the intersection of College, Laporte, Walnut, and Pine looked like in Fort Collins in the 1950s.

Best of all is the Disneyland City Hall. It's a direct copy of the old Larimer County Court house that was torn down in 1955 to make way for a new building.

The very first time any of the people from Fort Collins visited Disneyland in California, they found it to be spectacular. Disneyland was a magical place, filled with wonders beyond their wildest dreams. People loved Fantasyland, Frontierland, Tomorrowland, and Adventureland.

They were less impressed with Main Street, and took it for granted. They quickly passed by all the buildings with a feeling that they had seen them all before like they were street from their hometown, and that is exactly what it is.

So today, when people from Fort Collins visit Disneyland, or Disney World, or any other of the Disneyland's in Europe or Japan, they see Main Street. It's just the way Harper Goff saw it as a young boy. There is nothing like going all over the world and finding out you have come home.

Fort Collins really is...Main Street, USA.

*Hughes Stadium
by Paul Nielsen*

One word describes the 1960s in Fort Collins. Growth! All of the preliminaries were over. Northern Colorado had prepared itself with an expanded water supply, the university had prepared by expanding itself, and the city's business district was gearing up. The floodgates were open and people were pouring into town. The entire decade was a kaleidoscope of breathless growth in all directions. As a people, we were infected with the heady spirit of achievement. It was as if the city had been living in a kind of perpetual adolescence for too many years. Not since the exciting days of the 1870s when Fort Collins was brand new, with a railroad to put the town on the map and a feeling that you could accomplish anything, had the people felt as they did now. In the 60s, Fort Collins began to flex its muscles, and it was an exciting time for everyone.

## The 1960s At a Glance

1960  • Poudre School District is reorganized.

1961  • An Atlas Intercontinental Ballistic Missile passes through town to much fanfare, on its way to its launch site northwest of town.

1962  • The hometown invention, the Water-Pik begins production in Fort Collins.

1964  • Fort Collins celebrates its centennial.

1965  • State Dry Goods fire kills Fire Chief Cliff Carpenter

1967  • WWV time station is built outside of Fort Collins and begins broadcasting time to the world.

1968  • Hughes Stadium is dedicated.

1969  • City votes to end liquor sales restrictions.

# The Numbers Start Adding Up
## 1960-1969

## POPULATION

| 1960 | 25,027 |
|------|--------|
| 1969 | 43,000 |

Up 71.8%

## RETAIL SALES

| 1960 | $44.9 million |
|------|---------------|
| 1969 | $88.3 million |

Up 96.6%

## MANUFACTURING AND PROCESSING EMPLOYMENT

| 1960 | 1,068 |
|------|-------|
| 1969 | 3,411 |

Up 210%

## ENROLLMENT-CSU

| 1960 | 6,131 |
|------|--------|
| 1969 | 16,252 |

Up 165%

## ENROLLMENT-POUDRE R-1

| 1960 | 7,050 |
|------|--------|
| 1969 | 12,191 |

Up 72.9%

By the beginning of 1960, the population of Fort Collins had grown to 25,027 people. This was 10,000 more people than just ten years before. But it was only the tip of the iceberg for what was about to happen in the next ten years. Growth meant prosperity and Fort Collins had much too recent memories of what it was like to be poor, to have a third of the houses in town vacant, and no new business enterprises. No one was going to do much complaining that there was anything inherently wrong with the new growth scenario.

All the vitality of the area was starting to attract new business and industry. Some of it was home grown and part of it came to town because of the attractions it offered.

One of the homegrown companies was Aqua-Tec, better known as the manufacturer of the Water Pik. The revolutionary dental appliance traces its roots back to 1958 when Fort Collins resident John Mattingly was talking to his dentist, Dr. Gerald Moyer. Moyer said that what was needed was a mechanical tool for cleaning between teeth and along the gum line. It would be a wonderful supplement to the toothbrush. Mattingly, a mechanical engineer went to work on the project. By 1962, he had perfected the oral hygiene device and manufacturing began in a small house with three employes.

THE WATER PIK. A Fort Collins invented homegrown success. The revolutionary dental appliance has been a major employer since 1962. (Courtesy Fort Collins Public Library)

The Water Pik was a huge success. In 1962, the company moved to its present location on East Prospect. Production increased 415% the next year and another 170% the following year. The economic impact on Fort Collins was significant. Not only did the company give the city a new

**45**

million dollar tax base, but most of the eventual 1,000 employees came from the Fort Collins area. Growth has been steady and the company has successfully marketed any number of water technology products over the last 40 years. The newest product is a battery operated dental flosser. The complete line of Water Piks, shower massagers, and other products are sold by the millions all over the world, but the company is a Fort Collins original.

Another Fort Collins company that expanded during the 1960s was Woodward Governor. It had come to town on a small scale in 1955, but now the Rockford, Illinois company started moving major operations to the Fort Collins. Their original site on Jefferson Street proved to be too small and so another site was selected on the south side of town at the corner of Drake and Lemay.

Woodward governor is a heavy machinery manufacturing facility. It makes engine governors for ships, locomotives, trucks, pipeline stations and for the big machinery at Cape Canaveral, Florida. It employees about 600 workers in Fort Collins today.

*A GOOD NEIGHBOR. Woodward Governor has been a community supporter since 1955. Its grounds are among the most beautifully landscaped in the community. It's annual Christmas decorations are enjoyed by thousands. (Courtesy Style Magazine)*

When it was announced that the plant was moving south into what was essentially a residential area, some of the neighbors were concerned. Others said they would not buy a home that was so close to a big factory. But the fears turned out to be unfounded. Woodward

Governor is one of the most beautiful areas in Fort Collins. It's surrounded by a huge expanse of trees and lush grass in a park-like setting. You would never know that it was a big manufacturing plant at all. It's a wonderful neighbor and every year thousands of people drive through the grounds to see the extensive outdoor Christmas displays. In fact, the corner of Drake and Lemay has been studied by city planners all over the U.S. as an example of compatible land use on four corners - shopping center, church, manufacturing, and residential.

The principal industry of Fort Collins in the 1960s and continuing even to the present day is residential and commercial construction. All kinds of construction, homes, businesses, commercial buildings, retail stores, restaurants, and university buildings. It has been one of the key muscular engines that have provided the thousands of jobs responsible for Fort Collins' continuing prosperity.

# The Developers Develop

When the Korean War ended in 1953, a 23 year old man came home from the war and moved to Fort Collins to open a new branch of the family lumber yard business. The company had purchased the old Gould lumberyard after the death of the owner. The young man was to be the manager of the business and receive $300 a month for his work. From that moment on, Fort Collins would never be the same again. Just as some of the early pioneers of the Poudre Valley had made an enormous impact on the establishment of the city in 1873, so did this man have the same effect exactly 80 years later.

The similarities between the early settlers and this renaissance settler were striking. They were both hard working, honest, and deeply respected by their peers. The early pioneers felt a sense of community citizenship and worked hard for the betterment of the city. This man felt the same.

When you review the list of the most important people in Fort Collins history, Joseph Mason, Bill Stover, Abner Loomis, and B.F. Hottel, Bob Everitt can be added as a contemporary pioneer.

The Everitt family had been in the lumberyard business for many years. Bob Everitt had worked in the business since he was 11 years old. He was well schooled in

CITY BUILDER. Bob Everitt has been a part of the entire half-century of growth and prosperity of Fort Collins. He has been instrumental in making the city what it is today. (Courtesy The Everitt Companies)

*BASE OF OPERATIONS. The Everitt Lumber Company was the seed from which all the many development projects began, including homes, commercial buildings, and the Foothills Fashion Mall. (Courtesy The Everitt Companies)*

the field when he got to Fort Collins. The Lumberyard was located in the 200 block of North College. Shortly after taking over the lumberyard, he opened a paint store in the old Union Pacific train depot on Jefferson Street.

The corporate offices for Everitt Lumber Company were moved to Fort Collins in 1961. Arriving with the corporate office was the senior of the Everitt family, Bob's father Les. He was a stately gentleman, very soft-spoken, but very sincere. The four lumberyards grew to 15 by 1983. By this time, the energy created by developing new subdivisions and

*THE FIRST MALL. Built in 1964, the University Mall was Fort Collins first enclosed mall. It was a project of Mae Tiley and her son Bill, who developed many homes and businesses. (Courtesy Fort Collins Public Library)*

other commercial ventures made the lumberyards less main stream to the Everitt visions. All of them were sold to Weyerhaeuser in 1983.

It wasn't long before Bob Everitt realized the potential in the home building industry and soon was involved. CSU had decided to move its agronomy farm from its location in the section of town that was bounded by Stover, Elizabeth, Prospect, and the street that was then known as Hospital Road. CSU put the 120 acres up for sale to the highest bidder in 1957. Everitt bid $2,500 an acre and Mae Tiley and her son Bill bid $2,510 an acre. In the end, Everitt and Tiley became partners in the development and platted a new subdivision they called University Acres. Tiley became the managing partner for the project.

The original idea was to build homes on the entire plot of land, and so that's the way they platted it. However, soon many other people and institutions became interested in getting involved. The master plan was revised to accommodate churches, a nursing home, a medical center across from the hospital, and a site for the new Lesher Junior High School. Everitt and Tiley made the changes and continued to build homes on the remaining land.

*LESHER JUNIOR HIGH. Named for the Superintendent of Schools David B. Lesher who presided over the growth of the Poudre School District in the 1950s and 60s. (Courtesy Fort Collins Public Library)*

These homes were somewhat more upscale than the smaller homes being built on the west side of town by Alvin Miller and others. Those homes were in the $15 to $20 thousand range, while the University Acres homes had price tags that averaged $30 to $40 thousand.

The subdivision took ten years to develop. Everitt and Tiley had to work around the continuing work CSU was doing on the land, and to coordinate with the University while it was still irrigating the growing crops.

The demand for housing continued unabated. The same year

University Acres was initiated; Everitt bought 80 acres along Stuart Street that went south to Columbia and from Stover to Hospital Road. He called this subdivision Indian Hills and, along with Darrel Blake he started building more houses. As with many of the subdivisions in Fort Collins, Everitt built some of the houses himself, and sold some of the lots to local builders to develop on their own.

Indian Hills abutted Tiley's South College Heights on the west. It was separated by Stover Street, which had been set aside as a major north/south street. However, there was a problem in connecting Stover between Stuart and Prospect. First, some older homes had been built along Stuart several years before. One or two of them lay right in the path of what should have been the right of way for Stover Street. Next, the Sunset Drive-in Theatre was still in operation on Stuart. There was

also the matter of Spring Creek that ran along Stuart Street and would have to be crossed with several bridges. Finally, there was the new problem created by the construction of Barton School right at the spot where Stover should have been extended.

AN UNFORTUNATE LOCATION. Barton School was built on Prospect St. Its placement made it impossible to extend Stover St. as a southern arterial, and produced future traffic problems. (Courtesy of John Clarke

All of these issues made it difficult to extend Stover Street south of Prospect. At the time, it seemed like a minor glitch, but it turned out to have a major effect on the movement of people in Fort Collins. Stover Street would have been the half-mile point between College and Lemay. It would have provided a main arterial for cars and traffic moving north and south. This was critically important since the majority of the growth was occurring along this corridor. Families who lived in the new subdivisions of the area were forced to College Avenue or Lemay. Both of those streets, and particularly College Avenue, degraded into a morass of traffic very early in the growth cycle. This caused people to begin to ponder growth as a negative. It wasn't the growth that bothered them, it was the traffic.

Of course, none of this had anything to do with Bob Everitt or Bill Tiley. They had built on both sides of Prospect Street to meet the demand for housing. But the intervening block between Prospect and Stuart was outside of their subdivision boundaries.

One of the most interesting outcomes of this collaboration and the construction of homes along the south corridor was the street that had been known for many years, simply as Hospital Road (Poudre Valley Hospital was located on it). Further south it was just county road 13. Well, Bob Everitt and Bill Tiley got together and decided to give the road another name. They chose a mix of the names of Everitt's father, Les, and Tiley's mother Mae. It came out Lemay, and that's how the street got its name.

Meanwhile, Tiley was busy with a new enterprise of his own. This was Thunderbird subdivision just south of his development of South College Heights, across Drake. It was all built beginning in the late 60s. Tiley got a bargain on the land, paying about $1,500 an acre.

Everitt tackled his most ambitious construction project in the late 60s. This was the opening of the Parkwood subdivision. He bought 160 acres of farmland east of Lemay, between Drake and Stuart for about $2,000 an acre. The land included the lake that is at the corner of Drake and Lemay. In those days it was known as "Stink Pond." That's because it didn't have an outlet and the water just sat there and stagnated. The lake was filled with algae and weeds, and it smelled. One of the needs of the housing development was to reclaim the lake and make it a more presentable amenity for a housing subdivision.

*PERFECT SETTING. Parkwood Lake is a visual delight for both homeowners and commuters at the corner of Drake and Lemay. It's on one corner of the most unique intersection in Fort Collins. (Courtesy of John Clarke)*

PROTOTYPE OF MIXED USE. The corner of Drake and Lemay is an example of commercial, residential, and industrial land use in one area. It is used as a model for ideal development. (Courtesy The Mitchell Company)

Parkwood was mostly upscale homes, the best that had been built in Fort Collins in the modern age. Around the lake, was the choice building sites, some of them on as much as one acre of ground. These homes became the showplace for good living in Fort Collins for the next several years.

Part of the development included some townhomes and a group of apartments. This made the total density of the subdivision pretty high, which suited both the city and the buying public. With a fairly large number of families able to live in Parkwood in the combination of regular sized lots and multiple family dwellings, it compacted the area and made commuting to work and schools more convenient. It was a market driven development since a lot of people liked the idea of a Parkwood address, but not the drudgery of having to take care of a large lawn.

As it turned out, the corner of Drake and Lemay was to become a showcase for the new idea of mixed zoning. On one corner was the pretty lake with the beautiful houses built around it. On another corner was the expansive First Christian Church. On another corner was the Scotch Pines Shopping Center with a grocery store, and many convenience stores and offices. And on the final corner was a big manufacturing plant, carefully disguised as Woodward Governor with its wide expanses of trees and grass. It looked wonderful. It still does, and the people love it.

## Fairway Estates Breaks the Mold

Subdivision construction in the United States since the end of World War II had been pretty one-dimensional. Hundreds, even thousands of homes were built in an area. Along the fringes of the sprawling subdivisions were the commercial areas with the service centers that provided the conveniences to the residents. Their principal drawback was that it almost always required the use of a car to access these commercial centers. Moreover, multiple family areas were completely separate from both the single family homes and the retail centers. Everybody was driving everywhere.

UNIQUE DESIGN. Fairway Estates was the first example of estate lot planning in a park-like setting in Fort Collins. Still one of the most beautiful subdivisions in the city. (Courtesy Style Magazine)

Some of the developers in Fort Collins had adopted the practice of sprinkling parks, or open areas around the homes to provide some recreation and to give a little separation between residences. These came to be known as greenbelts. The Everitt Companies had begun using some of these upgrades in the Parkwood Subdivision.

In the early 1960s, a totally different kind of subdivision was devised in Fort Collins. It was the brainchild of Gordon Walker, and he called it Fairway Estates. Walker purchased 160 acres at the intersection of College Avenue and Harmony Road. At the time, it was a full three miles out of town, and in the country. Walker and his partner Loren Dilsaver designed a park with homes placed in it, rather than a subdivision of homes that included a park. This subtle distinction produced a whole new paradigm.

First Walker designed two large lakes through the center of the land. Around this he planned a par 3, 9 hole golf course. Mixed in with the lakes and the golf course he placed walking paths and pocket park alcoves. With all this designed, he then placed home lots in the midst of the expansive park. The lots were huge. They ranged from half acre to 3 acre parcels. Strict building code covenants were established for prospective home builders to make Fairway Estates very upscale. The entire subdivision was sold out in record time, although Walker's friends said to him, "Gordon, why do you want to build a subdivision clear out there in the country?" The family was later to say that the only mistake they made at Fairway Estates was not holding on to the quarter mile of commercial frontage on College Avenue and Harmony Road for about twenty more years.

# Growing up in Fort Collins

The opening of the 1960s decade was an exciting time. It was a perfect environment for the Baby Boom generation. Young people in Fort Collins didn't always see it that way. Perhaps they were a little self-conscious about how small a town it was and always wanted it to be bigger. There was so little to do, they thought. None of the trappings of a metropolitan center had yet arrived in Fort Collins. They thought their hometown was mostly devoid of any kind of sophistication and the only way to get it was to get bigger. Now that the city had a population of 25,000 people, the youngsters believed they had achieved some level of respectability. It wasn't huge, but there were certainly more opportunities than there had been ten years before.

The young people were also of the opinion that the city had no significant heritage or history of any note. They couldn't remember anybody talking much about the past. It was a shock to find out that a real "fort" had once existed in town, but they had no idea where it had stood, what it was there for, or what it looked like. When they finally learned where the fort had been located, they were devastated to learn that this site was now the location of the city dump. It only confirmed their suspicions that Fort Collins was nothing, had always been nothing and the only way for it to be something was to grow up and become larger so that it could acquire things.

That's why the beginning of the 1960s was so much fun for the young people who were the reasons why families had chosen to migrate to suburbia in the first place. They enjoyed a tremendous amount of freedom in a community that was regarded as very safe. When the weekend rolled around, there was always an excitement in the air. During the fall, there were high school football games on Friday night and CSU games on Saturday. From then until March, the kids went to the high school and college basketball games. The events were always sold out. Everybody went.

12. *TEENAGE HANGOUT. Club Tico, in City Park, was the place to go on the weekends for teens growing up in the 50s and 60s in Fort Collins. (Courtesy Fort Collins Public Library)*

After the games, they went to a place called Club Tico. It was in City Park in the building next to the pool. The whole second floor was a youth center with pool tables, pinball machines, a snack bar, a dance floor, and a bandstand. It was run by volunteers from the high school and was only for high school kids. The man in charge was Mr. Warner. Notice that he was a Mister. He was never anybody other than "Mr. Warner." He was the shop teacher. Nobody messed around with Mr. Warner. Club Tico was always fun, never out of control...never. It was open on Friday and Saturday nights.

One of the favorite pastimes of just about everybody was "cruising main." This means exactly the same thing as it does today, only shorter. The cruising route went from center parking downtown, south to Prospect to Morrie's In 'n Out. Morrie's was Fort Collins first drive-through restaurant. It was located about, where the service station is today at the corner of Prospect and College. It was incredibly popular. It didn't have a restaurant to go into, it didn't have a walk up. It was just a drive through. There was hardly a time in which there was less than 20 cars snaking through the drive through lane like a big python. It was unique because of the drive through feature, and the fact that you could order your "Paul Bunyan

FIRST DRIVE IN RESTAURANT. Morrie's In and Out, at the corner of College and Prospect was a popular spot for an emerging mobile community. (Courtesy Fort Collins Public Library)

Burger" on a speaker hung out on a post. This was true space age stuff, and very much in keeping with a young person's idea of what a modern metropolis ought to look like. Morrie used to say that he could handle one car a minute. This meant that a visit to the drive in restaurant was something less than fast food, especially if there were 30 cars ahead of you at the time. However, people had a somewhat different concept of time in those days, and waiting for something was less of an irritation. In fact, they turned the long waits into a social occasion. The young men learned early that you get hungrier waiting in line than what you ordered clear back at the entrance. So, it was very common for a car with five teenagers in it to order 15 Paul Bunyan Burgers, with fries and cokes. There was never anything left over.

Somewhere around 1959, an A&W drive in was built, a little bit further south on College Avenue at about Spring Creek, on the east side of the road. This was superior to Morrie's. The kids could pull in, wait for the waitress to come out and take their order, at which time they would hassle her mercilessly, and then get out of their cars and go socialize with everybody else until their food arrived.

From the youngster's perspective, Fort Collins hit the big time in 1960. McDonalds opened a restaurant on South College in the middle of a cornfield. The University Mall had not yet been built. McDonalds was all there was clear out there in the country. It looked a lot different than it does today, and it must have been one of the first ones in the country. There was no drive through. It was a walk up. It had real neon golden arches, the picture of that hamburger with a face and hands and feet, and a sign which said, "Over 300,000 served." No kidding. They changed the sign a lot. The young people would remark that it would be a big day when they could put up on their flashing neon sign that a million McDonald hamburgers had been sold. It was pretty naive of them. The hamburgers were 15 cents, and fries were a dime. That meant you could eat six hamburgers and a bag of fries for one dollar. For growing teenagers, it happened often.

# An Exploding University

The university continued its massive build-up. By 1962, school year enrollment had grown to 7,304 students. During the decade, those numbers would double to 16,252, by 1969. By the middle of the decade, more that $20 million had been spent on new facilities and buildings.

CSU dedicated its new $1.8 million Engineering Research Center on the school's foothills campus two miles west of town. It became known as the hydrology lab. Senator Gordon Allott was present for the dedication and said, "The center was designed to serve as a focus for water

SEAT OF KNOWLEDGE. *The Morgan Library on the CSU campus is the center for learning and research for the students and faculty at the university. (Courtesy Style Magazine)*

resources and its studies will be of state and national importance." He was right about that. In just a few years students from all over the world were flocking to Fort Collins to learn all about water. 70% of the world's population lives in sparse or semi-arid water conditions. The ways that Colorado had rewritten the laws on water resources, the way that northern Colorado had learned how to manage water through the Colorado-Big Thompson project, and the way that CSU had learned to teach the concepts, became the standard for water law and management world wide. CSU had its first big-time international connection.

A bigger university meant more study and research was done by the student body. This meant a bigger library was needed. The Morgan Library was built in 1966 with Federal funds and answered the criticism that had been leveled at the university by the North Central Association of Colleges and Secondary Schools. The students agreed. The old library on the oval was so inadequate that you almost had to wait in line to get in, and when you did, the book you wanted was either checked

*MANY MOMENTS of excitement have been seen at CSU's Moby Gym. Athletic contests, concerts, and special events have all been a part of the life of this facility, built in 1966. (Courtesy Style Magazine)*

out or didn't exist in the system.

In 1966, Moby Gym was completed at a cost of $4.2 million. It was built with state funds. This was handy since the CSU basketball team was going through one of its most successful eras under the coaching of Jim Williams. In the 1960s, the Rams went to the NIT or the NCAA tournaments six times. The team got to the elite eight in 1968 in the NCAA national tournament before losing to Drake. Bill Green was the star during this period and was CSU's only 1st team All-American. He was drafted by the Boston Celtics, but didn't like to travel and was

*GO RAMS! The 30,000 seat Hughes Stadium is the home of the CSU Ram football team. Built in 1968 at the edge of the foothills, the stadium is a located just under the colorful "A." (Courtesy of John Clarke)*

afraid of flying. He went on to become a very successful high-school teacher and administrator.

Also coming on line in 1968 was the new 30,000 seat Hughes stadium. In that year, CSU became part of the Western Athletic Conference. Hughes Stadium was named for legendary coach Harry Hughes who lead the Aggies to 8 conference championships between 1911 and 1941.

# CSU. Creator of the Peace Corps

In the past 40 years, more than 150,000 Americans have served in the Peace Corps in over 130 countries around the world. It is one of the most recognizable and successful of all government programs. President John F. Kennedy initiated it shortly after his inauguration in 1961. You will be fascinated to hear the story of how the Peace Corps came to be, and you will be surprised to learn that the Peace Corps was actually created in Fort Collins at Colorado State University.

This story begins in the late 1950s. U.S. Senator Hubert Humphrey was mesmerized by the concept of voluntary Foreign Service by Americans. He had one staff person who did nothing else but work on the idea. Reams of testimony were taken exploring the concept. The principal was based on the overwhelming success of the Marshall Plan for Europe after World War II. Humphrey, and others, wondered if it was possible to apply that principle of aid to all of the underdeveloped and needy countries of the world.

*FATHER OF THE PEACE CORPS. Dr. Maurice Albertson was the Director of Research and Development at CSU in the 50s and 60's. His work made the Peace Corps possible. (Courtesy of Dr. Albertson)*

Congress had an interest too. In the House Congressman Henry Reuss from Wisconsin, and Senator Thomas Neuberger from Oregon, both sponsored bills that address this and other issues having to do with foreign aid. The result was the passage of the Foreign Assistance Act in 1960.

Imbedded in that legislation was a provision for $10,000 to be spent to study the feasibility of a volunteer group of workers to go around the world helping people. It was actually the fourth point of the legislation and it came to be known simply as "Point Four."

The scene now shifts to Fort Collins were a student at Colorado State University saw the provision for the study and its $10,000 price tag in a news report. He brought the matter up with one of his professors, Dr. Maurice Albertson, in the Civil Engineering Department. The news could not have fallen on better ears. Dr. Albertson was, at that time, the Director of Research for the entire university. CSU President Bill Morgan had asked him to do the job in 1958 and Albertson had accepted on the condition that his research fundraising would extend beyond the College of Engineering and include all the departments at the school.

This study the government wanted to conduct seemed like exactly the kind of project that would allow a research program to include the Department of Social Sciences. It was also a subject that Dr. Albertson knew something about. Just a few years before he had been instrumental in the establishment of the Asian Institute of Technology. It had been the pet project of the President of Thailand who was trying to start a hydrology program on the Mekong River. Albertson had been all over the world getting support from other countries for the institute and was well acquainted with grass roots programs for 3rd World and underdeveloped nations. He was also a familiar face in Washington, D.C. He traveled there two or three times a month talking to government officials about grants for research projects.

So, Albertson embarked on a campaign to get the grant to study the idea of a Peace Corps. He was aided in this by a member of his department,

60

Pauline Birky, who was just back from two years in Iran where she had worked directly with the people of that country to help solve some of their problems.

As luck would have it, Albertson was scheduled to be in Washington just a week after the announcement of the $10,000 had been made. He was going to a conference on International Development. One of the speakers at that conference was Congressman Harry Reuss himself, the author of the bill that created the grant in the first place. Reuss told everybody that he was due back on the hill for an important vote and couldn't stay, so Albertson asked if he couldn't ride back to the capital with him in the cab. During that 15 minute ride, Albertson told the congressman all about the experience that CSU had with working on foreign assistance programs. Ruess was intrigued and took Albertson to his office where he gave him stacks of papers that contained every idea that anybody had ever had about the notion of a Peace Corps. Albertson brought it all home to Fort Collins.

Once back at CSU, Albertson and Birky pulled together every professor on campus who had any experience in working with people in foreign countries. There were over 30 people who had, and the two of them wrung out every drop of information they knew.

From this study came the basic design for the modern Peace Corps.

When Albertson submitted his proposal to get the $10,000 grant, he found out that no less than six major research organizations and institutions had already applied. They included New York, and Stanford Universities. Fledgling CSU, just three years into actually being a university was small potatoes in the mix.

Undaunted, Albertson began an intensive lobbying campaign with the two main decision-makers for the program in the State Department and at AID. At least once a week, from March through September of 1960, he sent them updates. CSU was continuing to do research on the program,

*Conditions in host countries are often difficult and challenging. A Peace Corps volunteer faces them all with the knowledge that they can make a difference. (Courtesy of Dr. Maurice Albertson)*

although they didn't have the grant.  By this time Albertson had gone all out and had gotten $30,000 more dollars from other sources to add to his war chest.  This zeal on his part, plus the true expertise that Albertson and his colleagues had in the field made the difference.  CSU got the grant.

An important piece of the puzzle was completed in the summer of 1960.  Two men were just coming out of a private organization called the International Voluntary Services.  They planned to attend CSU in the fall.  Albertson learned of their work in Foreign Service and asked the men if they could come to Fort Collins and work with his group during the summer.  The men agreed and turned out to be walking encyclopedias on how volunteers should work in the field.  From this information, Albertson got the prototype on how the Peace Corps should function.

Albertson knew how the Peace Corps was going to operate in the field.  He had learned that from all the input he had received.  What he didn't know was from where the volunteers were going to come.  He sent out questionnaires to a large number of schools to find out who would be interested in volunteering.

One of the most interesting calls he got was from Walter Ruether, President of the AFL-CIO Labor Union.  Ruether was fascinated with the idea and wanted a sample of the questionnaire to send to all his members.

*VOLUNTEERS ABROAD. On the job projects are often simple additions to the life of a remote village. This chicken coop was something the people needed, so the Peace Corps volunteer built it. (Courtesy Dr. Maurice Albertson)*

A few weeks later he called back and was very distressed. He said he couldn't understand it, but that there was absolutely no interest whatsoever on the part of his membership. Albertson said he was sorry and couldn't understand it either.

As the data came back from the other schools, a picture began to form. The greatest and most enthusiastic interest came from the private universities. The poorest response came from the state land grant universities. Albertson has since developed a theory on this. He believes that the response was so poor from the labor unions because most of their workers were just one generation away from being immigrants themselves. They were too busy trying to make a living in America to stop and go to a foreign country, maybe their own, and lend a hand. This was also true to a lesser degree at the land grant schools. They were one more generation removed from immigrant status and were still too engrossed in making a success of their own lives to volunteer. The private schools, however, were filled with students who had no real concept of poverty and need, and had both the time and the money to volunteer. That trend continues even until today.

The presidential campaign in 1960 was a very close affair. John Kennedy and Richard Nixon were running neck and neck and the outcome was very much in doubt, but the odds makers were giving the edge to Nixon. Hubert Humphrey knew that Kennedy needed an edge to give him the election. Humphrey had been keeping tabs on the fledgling Peace Corps concept. He continued to try and convince Kennedy to use it in his campaign. Kennedy was skeptical. Finally, Humphrey prevailed. On Oct 14th, Kennedy was scheduled to spend the night in Ann Arbor, Michigan. 3,000 students from the University of Michigan waited for his arrival scheduled for midnight. Kennedy was delayed until 2 AM, but there were still about 1,500 students waiting for him. Kennedy, tired and worn out from campaigning decided to give the Peace Corps idea a try, particularly since the press had gone to bed thinking that nothing else was going to happen that night. Kennedy announced the idea for the Peace Corps, and was astonished to see the students go completely crazy over the idea.

Humphrey encouraged Kennedy to use the idea in a major speech. Kennedy agreed and on the near eve of the election gave a final address at the Cow Palace in San Francisco that heavily featured the concept of the Peace Corps. That audience loved the idea too, and so did the country. Kennedy got a bump in the ratings from the speech, and won the election.

Now the way this story ends is that the very first thing Kennedy did after he was inaugurated in January 1961 was to appoint Sargent Shriver to be the head of his new Peace Corps.  Shortly thereafter, Albertson remembers that Shriver called him at about 2 o'clock in the morning. He apologized for calling so late but said that he had been on the phone the whole night and that he had just gotten to Albertson's name. Albertson said it was quite all right and wanted to know what he could do for the new Peace Corps Director.  Shriver wanted Albertson to get on a plane that night and fly to Washington to brief him on the details of the study and the operational plans for the Corps.  He was highly annoyed that Albertson put him off for four days before getting to Washington.

Through Shriver, the new president implemented the CSU plan in its entirety, with two exceptions.  The first exception was that Albertson had recommended that a course of study, subsidized by the government just like R.O.T.C. be used as a training vehicle for volunteers.  Shriver hated that idea and rejected it out of hand.  The second exception was that the study had recommended an independent evaluation and monitoring program to report directly to the Shriver on how the volunteers were doing on the job.  Shriver didn't like that either and said that this job could just as easily done by the press.

So, that is how the Peace Corps came to be.  The origins of that exciting program have been clouded in obscurity for nearly 40 years.  But now you know, so to speak, the rest of the story.

# The Centennial

The city was really feeling its oats.  It was very proud of what it was accomplishing and didn't miss any chances to celebrate.  A wonderful event appeared early in the decade.  Somebody figured out that we were getting close to the 100-year mark since the establishment of the Fort. This produced a committee to explore the possibilities of having a commemoration of the event.  Some people wondered why we were doing this on the occasion of the establishment of the Fort instead of the city itself.  Quite a few people thought that we should wait to hold the celebration until we arrived at the centennial of the city in 1973.  But the logic went that the name "Fort Collins, " no matter what the form of it was, should be the benchmark.  Since the Fort was established in August 1864, that meant we were a hundred years old.

Actually, it was a little hoax that we were playing on ourselves.  The citizens were so proud, so excited about their growing town that most didn't want to wait another nine years to tell everybody how wonderful we were.  It's likely that they were trying to shake off a feeling of inferiority that had been pervasive for many years.  Living in the shadow of a

CENTENNIAL SUPPORT. *Fort Collins Centennial creator Jim Guyer receives check from Columbia Saving's Don Stuart while PR director Peggy Reed looks on and Phil Walker covers the event on KCOL. (Courtesy Fort Collins Public Library)*

colorful Colorado history that had seemed to mostly pass them by was always on their minds. They didn't like playing second fiddle to Denver, or to some extent, Greeley, which was still considerably larger than Fort Collins and more prosperous. Weld County was producing millionaires in agriculture and it was hard for Fort Collins to compete on that basis. Now, the city had a few things going for itself, and just couldn't miss the opportunity to crow a little.

The Fort Collins Centennial Commission was established in 1963. The prime mover for the Commission was James Guyer. He was the man who got all the committees organized and waded through the mass of planning and details to hold the centennial the following year.

Guyer's original plan was to have events and activities throughout the year. This turned out to be more than he could handle or what the city was interested in doing. One of Guyer's biggest problems was to get people to look up from their work long enough to take part in the celebration. There was also the problem of not having enough people in town with any memories of a Fort Collins gone by. Just as today, most of the people in Fort Collins came here from somewhere else. They didn't have the historical perspective and the decades of living in Fort Collins to get them very enthused. Moreover, the mind set of that time was focused on the future, not the past. Fort Collins residents were busy building and celebrating the wonderful Fort Collins that was yet to come. The past seemed like an irrelevant anachronism.

A final complication of having a big centennial celebration was the simple fact that most people didn't have a clue about the history of our town. The old-timers didn't seem to talk about it very much. The last book on the history of the area had been written clear back in 1911, when Ansel Watrous wrote his voluminous History of Larimer County. Since that time, it was as if the whole community had lived like rabbits. Everyday was a new world. The resurgence in an interest in Fort Collins history didn't come until much later when some people started writing about it.

The Centennial Commission labored along and finally announced that the celebration would begin on the Memorial Day Weekend, and conclude on August 20th, the date of the signing of the order establishing the Fort Collins Military Reservation.

Memorial Day weekend, 1964 arrived, along with miserable weather. Most of the time the weather is pretty predictable. It clouds up, rains for an hour, and then the sun comes out again. Not this time. The weather turned bad on Thursday. The clouds rolled in and never left. It was very unusual. It would rain for a while, then it would drizzle for hours. The rest of the time it was gloomy, dark, and looked like it was going to rain again any minute. After all the work and planning, great sections of the scheduled events had to be cancelled, postponed or changed. It was discouraging to all the hundreds of people who had worked to bring this grand beginning of the Centennial to fruition.

But the ceremonies managed to take place for the most part. The weather was good enough on Thursday, May 28th for the delivery of Volume One of the Centennial booklet. Both Volume One, and the second volume published after the Centennial events to make them a part of history were underwritten by Columbia Savings for $4,000. The booklets were delivered by helicopter, a very unusual event since a helicopter had hardly ever been seen in Fort Collins, to the playground of St. Joseph's School near downtown. The children loved it. The booklets were then transported by horsedrawn carriage provided by J.D. Forney to the 14 merchants who would serve as the sales outlets. The event was carried live, on KCOL radio.

All of the main events were supposed to happen on Sunday, the 30th, but the weather made everybody scramble to make other arrangements. The official kickoff address by Supreme Court Justice Byron White, where he eulogized deceased members of the community and spoke inspirationally about our centennial, was supposed to be out on the big grassy area west of the student center on the CSU campus. The reason it was there was because just before that happened the famous Golden Knights parachute team from the U.S. Army was going to do a skydiving exhibition. The rain made it impossible for the skydivers to perform. This was a huge disappointment for everyone. Skydiving in those days was a very thrilling and new thing. A huge crowd was expected to see this wondrous event where people actually fell out of the air for thousands of feet before opening their parachutes. It was beyond most people's understanding to imagine such death-defying magic. The cancellation of the jump was a crushing blow.

Justice White was forced indoors into the student center ballroom, as was the appearance of the CSU Symphonic Band and Community Chorus. These groups were playing some original works that had been written by local composers just for the occasion. The people still turned out for the performance, while the rain continued to fall.

GRAND PARADE. On of the biggest in history, the Centennial Parade went down College Avenue on the 4th of July. (Courtesy Fort Collins Public Library)

The second part of the centennial celebration was on the 4th of July. The weather was just perfect. It started with a huge parade downtown. One of the biggest parades ever held in Fort Collins. There were floats and bands and old cars and horses and marching units. That afternoon there was a big concert by the Fort Carson band, plus a lot of games. It was held on the oval at CSU and thousands of people attended. Across campus, they had a beef and buffalo barbecue with twelve serving lines running to feed all the people. Then everyone settled down to an hour

ON THE OVAL. *The community gathered for an outdoor concert and a 4th of July fireworks finale. The only time the 4th has been celebrated outside of city park. (Courtesy Fort Collins Public Library)*

long fireworks show. This is the only time in history in which the city fireworks occurred somewhere else besides City Park.

At the end of July, the Fort Collins Little Theatre Group presented a production called "Pioneer Panorama." This was a show that highlighted the most important events in the first one hundred years. It was held at the CSU Student Center Theatre over three nights and to sellout crowds.

The climax of the Fort Collins Centennial celebration was a huge banquet to honor all the living "old-timers" of the city and all the people who had worked on the Centennial Commission for the previous year. This was held on August 20th, the day in which Lt. Colonel William O. Collins had signed the order establishing the fort. There was a large contingent of dignitaries from the city, county and state present, plus many from the community. A special coin had been minted for the occasion and was either presented or sold to the banquet attendees. This was the end of the formal centennial celebration. Fort Collins enjoyed it, thought it was quaint, and then promptly went back to work.

# The State Dry Goods Fire

The decade was rolling along. Most of the news of the day was good news. Growth and prosperity were the signs of the times. But then an event occurred that caught everyone's attention. As with most of the big stories, this one was tragic and destructive and came unexpectedly without warning.

*A DOWNTOWN LANDMARK. The State Dry Goods Building was an impressive brick and stone building at the corner of College and Oak. Fort Collins biggest department store. (Courtesy Fort Collins Public Library)*

During most of the 1960's, Fort Collins' main business activity was still confined to downtown. The land where the Foothills Fashion Mall was built was still a farm owned by a family named Spencer. The chain stores Sears, Penny's, and the principle local businesses all were head-quartered within a block or two of the intersection of College and Mountain. The largest department store in town was called the State Dry Goods, and it was owned locally by the Johnson family. It was a grand two-story brick building at the corner of College and Oak, where the Oak Street Plaza is today, across from the post office facing College Avenue. Oak Street was still open to traffic across College Avenue and the old Post Office was still in operation.

Just after 9 p.m. on June 28, 1965, a short circuit occurred in an electrical box in one of the display windows facing College. Sparks from the short circuit rained down on the highly flammable clothes in the display window and a small fire began to burn.

The fire burned inside the State Dry goods building, uncontrolled and undetected for over an hour, until all of the oxygen in the building had been consumed. This caused the flames to go out, but the fire itself was a glowing, super-heated mass that was smoldering at several hundred degrees, waiting for a breath of fresh air to give it life again.

At 10:30 p.m., one of the huge, quarter-inch plate glass windows shattered, blowing glass clear across College Avenue. The fresh air rushed in and a huge backdraft caused the fire to violently reignite. The entire State Dry Goods building exploded in a jarring concussion that woke up half the town.

Within minutes, every piece of fire equipment in the entire city was racing toward downtown Fort Collins. Firefighters arrived to find the building and the entire corner of College and Oak, fully engulfed in flames that are shooting hundreds of feet into the air.

Also arriving, and setting up a mobile broadcast transmitter just west of the old Post Office on Oak street, was a 21 year old radio announcer who was caught with a live microphone for the next two hours

*"Once again, from downtown Fort Collins, this is Phil Walker with more of our continuing coverage of a major fire which has destroyed most of the State Dry Goods building at the corner of College and Oak.*

*For those of you who may be just joining us, let me bring you up to date on the events that have happened here tonight.*

*An all-alarm call for all available fire fighting units in Fort Collins, with support coming from as far away as Loveland and Wellington, was made at approximately 10:30 tonight when the State Dry Goods building suddenly erupted in a fireball of flame. Eyewitnesses say that the entire building seemed to explode like a bomb and that flames shot into the sky at least two hundred feet. By the time, that fire units arrived the building was completely engulfed in flames. The building houses, not only the State Dry Goods, but also a drug store and Bowen's BookStore. There are no people believed to have been inside any of the businesses when the fire broke out.*

*The fire has now been burning, out of control, for over an hour and a half. Police have cordoned off the entire downtown area from literally thousands of curious spectators who are lining the police barriers in hopes of seeing the fire.*

*The greatest danger, according to Fire Chief Cliff Carpenter, is that the fire will spread to the other buildings along the West Side of the 100 block of South College. Most of the buildings were built before the turn of the century, and the firewalls between them may not be enough to keep the fire from spreading.*

*The new snorkel truck with its 85-foot hydraulic boom is currently positioned above the fire on the north side of the building and is concentrating all of its water right on the firewall as a deterrent to the fire spreading down the street.*

*The cause of the fire is not known at this time.*

*The fire has now burned through both the basement and the second floor and a few minutes ago, just after midnight, the entire roof collapsed into the interior of the structure. All that remains of the building is the front along College Avenue and the exposed south side along Oak Street from the alley to College Avenue.*

*We are located just across the street on Oak, west of the Post Office. The south side of the State Dry goods building is a brick wall, about thirty feet high*

*THE TRAGIC MOMENT. A photographer snapped this picture just as the south wall of the State Dry Goods building collapsed. Fire Chief Cliff Carpenter is buried under tons of rubble. (Courtesy Fort Collins Public Library)*

*topped with heavy concrete masonry that sticks out a couple of feet. There are several windows on this wall and fire is shooting out of them. The heat, even from here, about a hundred feet away is intense.*

*Currently firefighters are working along the wall and have several hoses running through the open windows in hopes of getting to the main fire deeper inside the building. Fire Chief Cliff Carpenter is directing this work. In fact, a little while ago I saw him give one of his exhausted men a break on one of the hoses and man it himself. The fire is.......*

*My God, the entire wall has just collapsed! I saw two or three firemen running away from the falling bricks to just barely escape being crushed under all those tons of materials! But I think there were at least two men who were caught by the falling wall! Dozens of firemen, police, and even bystanders are now furiously digging in the rubble to try and uncover the men! We have no word on just who could be under that rubble or their condition, but Chief Carpenter was manning a hose just under the wall when it collapsed and I don't see him now! Ambulances are moving into position!*

*The firemen are now removing the last of the bricks so they can get whoever is trapped under there out! I can see one man who has been uncovered by the fire-*

*men, and he is now being placed on a stretcher! There is a tremendous amount of excitement near where the first fire-man was recovered! They are now taking a second man out of the rubble! I can't see....Oh my God! It's the Chief! Boy! I hope he's OK!"*

The Chief was not OK. He was pronounced dead on arrival at the Poudre Valley hospital. Fire Chief Cliff Carpenter is the only Fort Collins fireman who has ever died in the line of duty in our history. The second fireman was seriously injured, but recovered.

THE CHIEF. *Cliff Carpenter was the only Fort Collins Fireman to ever die in the line of duty. The city mourned the passing of the popular chief. (Courtesy Fort Collins Public Library)*

# An Evolving Social Structure

Fort Collins was blessed with especially able mayors during the decade of the 60s. Gene Frink, 1961-63, Harvey Johnson, 1963-67, Dr. Thomas Bennett, 1967-68, and Dr. Karl Carson, 1968-73. All of them were elected to the city council by a vote of the people, and then selected from their peers to serve as mayor. Although the post of mayor was ceremonial in nature, and the mayor didn't have any more votes than any other city council member, they all served as the emotional, social and political barometer of the city.

Gene Frink, an architect by trade, understood the early expansion of the subdivisions and worked to insure that they fit into a cohesive master plan. Harvey Johnson was an expert on water. Hardly a single council went by without him leading an effort to acquire more water to add to the Fort Collins reserves. It was a wise and prudent step to take, although Fort Collins had plenty of water at the time. Johnson knew that with a city growing as fast as Fort Collins was, there would soon come a time when the additional water supplies would be needed and vital. He was right. Finally, Dr. Karl Carson ended the decade and served into the next. He was mayor for five terms. He recognized the need for the city to make provisions for the cultural and physical infrastructure of Fort Collins to meet the demands of an expanding and increasingly affluent public.

THE WATER MAYOR. Harvey Johnson was known for his interest in acquiring more water for Fort Collins. Under his leadership, the city bought water for the future. (Courtesy Fort Collins Public Library)

The city was less successful in handling their administration. The venerable Guy Palmes, who served as City Manager for 23 years, longer than any other man in that office, retired in 1961. The city administration was rudderless. In quick succession, the city council hired and fired five city managers in the next ten years. This was an indicator of the state of upheaval that was beginning to grip the city. Growth had come so quickly, the city had grown so fast, change had occurred at such blinding speed, that nobody could keep up with it. Everybody had an opinion on how to manage all this growth in an orderly manner. The city council labored on and on, and the unwilling victims were often the hapless city managers.

The people of Fort Collins were kept busy deciding on city projects and city policies. In 1961, the people voted on repealing the liquor law, leash laws for dogs, fluoridation of city water and balloting at municipal elections. The dog leash law passed, the bond issue was squashed, fluoridation of water was defeated, and the city voters decided that liquor was still not something they wanted in Fort Collins.

Prohibition of alcohol was a raging issue in the 1880s and 90s. There was a lot of sentiment among the good and moral people of Fort Collins to outlaw it. A variety of restrictions were placed on the sale of liquor and then, systematically repealed over time. Finally, in 1893, a woman was elected to the city council on a platform of prohibition. The result was that the city went dry and was still dry in the 1960s, except for the sale of 3.2% beer.

It wasn't a universal prohibition in the area. Larimer County was not dry, and there were a considerable number of illegal bootleggers operating around the margins of the city. It was an uneasy truce.

The Charco-Broiler, just outside the city on Highway 14, opened in 1957. Their emphasis was on good food and good service. Owner Gib McGarvey believed that this was the key to a successful restaurant, with or without liquor. The fact that being able to buy a mixed drink was included in the package made for a very successful operation that continues right up until modern times. McGarvey certainly set the standard

POPULAR NIGHTSPOT. People flocked to the Safari Nightclub for dinner, dancing and a good time. Bob Swerer and his band played every weekend. (Courtesy Fort Collins Public Library)

for others who would follow.

Then a well respected and well liked man proposed to open a nightclub just outside of the city limits in 1963. The county commissioners granted a liquor license to Bob Swerer. He and his wife, Marion, opened a new era in Fort Collins nightlife.

It was called the Safari and it was located on Link Lane, in the county, but real close to just about everything in Fort Collins. Swerer was a popular native of Fort Collins whose singing was much treasured by the people. The Safari was definitely upscale. It had a very large dance floor and people would flock to the nightclub every weekend to dance to the music of Bob Swerer and his group. Marion was the talented and charming hostess. They served very good food.

In a very short time, the Safari became "the" place to go. It got so that you had to make reservations to get a table for dinner, a fact that was unheard of in Fort Collins. The place was packed every single night, and more so on the nights the band played. It also served mixed drinks. That feature was always understated, like it was just a part of the décor and no more notable than the stuffed heads of lions, zebras, gazelles and other African animals that decorated the walls. The atmosphere was fun, wholesome, and refined. The very best people in town were customers. It didn't take long for people to start asking questions about this antiquated and puritan law about alcohol and mixed drinks. Furthermore, the other restaurants were complaining that they couldn't compete with an establishment that got to sell liquor by the drink. Finally, the business community was pointing out that a lot of national chains were looking at Fort Collins to put in restaurants, but that they wouldn't do it if they couldn't sell mixed drinks. The city council took up the matter in 1965, but the proposal was defeated.

Undaunted, the pro-alcohol forces regrouped and began a campaign to get the matter put on a city election ballot. The process took four years. In the intervening time, the voters chose to put a tax on tobacco sales, which was a sort of demonstration that the people still had regard for public health. The city council seemed to show support for liquor sales by granting a 3.2% beer license to CSU in March 1969. The following month, after a heated debate and campaign, 78% of the registered voters went to the polls in the city elections and voted to repeal the prohibition of alcohol by a vote of 4,853 in favor and 2,691 opposed. The first, legally sold, drink in Fort Collins was served on August 10, 1969.

Other social issues were less amenable to solution. Opposition to the Vietnam War was heating up all over the country. The anti-war activity arrived in Fort Collins in 1967 when students and faculty at CSU joined with a group of local citizens to express their opposition to the war. The Larimer County Democratic Party joined in the descent.

An actual demonstration occurred in March 1968, when several hundred marchers, made up mostly of students and faculty, marched down College Avenue. They were heckled and harassed by townspeople. One man was so incensed that he tried to run down the protesters with his truck. Nobody was injured, but the police had to step in and use mace to disperse the crowd. It was an ugly scene and nobody went away happy.

# Readin' Writin' and Reorganization

No institution was more effected by the growth of Fort Collins than the school district. Not only was the population growing by leaps and bounds, but also the number of school age children, fueled by the prodigious baby boom, was growing exponentially. The schools struggled to keep up.

The first thing that was needed was a complete reorganization of the district. Up until 1960, Larimer County had been served by no less than 30 school districts. This was an unwieldy number and the much too difficult and expensive to administer. On July 1, 1960, the voters were asked to approve a reorganization plan. It passed, albeit narrowly. All the districts were consolidated into three; Poudre R-1, for Fort Collins, Thompson R2-J for Loveland, and Park District for Estes Park.

Poudre R-1 found itself administering 1,856 square miles. This included six mountain schools the district retained. Other schools were consolidated or closed. Laporte lost its high school and all the students were bused to Fort Collins High. However, Laporte high school was transformed into Cache la Poudre Junior High with an elementary school added later.

Enrollment at the schools went up like a rocket. In December 1960, there were 7,050 students in the district. By 1969, that number had risen to 12,191. This represented a 73% increase. Other numbers were equally impressive. In 1960, the district had 334 teachers. By 1969, the number was 718. Teacher salaries increased over three times in the decade.

*KIDS, KIDS, KIDS. Thousands of school age children flooded into Fort Collins schools. The school district labored to keep up. (Courtesy Style Magazine)*

Per student, spending went up as well. The per pupil cost in 1960 was $338. At the end of the 1960s the per pupil cost was $666. The state average that year was $661.

The total budget for the district tripled during the decade. In 1960, the district budget was $2.9 million. In 1969, the budget had gone up to nearly $9.8 million. The Federal government gave the district $6,009 in 1960. Ten years later, that number had gone up to $528,000. State funding increased from $656,000 in 1960, to just under two million dollars in 1969.

Big numbers, but it wasn't enough. The district was staggering under the load of students and was trying to build new schools as fast as they could get funding for them. This was no easy task. The voters were positively cranky about having to face a new bond issue almost every year. The district presented five bond issues to the voters in the 60s and got three of them approved. Approved were bond issues in 1961, 1966, and 1969 for a total of $25.7 million. The voters turned down bond issues in 1965 for a total $8.8 million.

*MORE SCHOOLS. 45 school projects were completed in the 1960s. Among them were many new elementary schools like Tavelli. (Courtesy Style Magazine)*

Schools built during the decade included; Bennett, O'Dea, Moore, Putnam, Tavelli, Bauder, Irish and Riffenburgh elementary schools, Lesher and Blevins junior highs, and Poudre High School. The district completed a total of 45 building projects during the decade.

The school district had 33 buses running 331,000 miles a year in 1960. At the end of 1969, the district was running 52 buses over a half million miles a year.

And the kids just kept coming.

# What Time Is It?

If you want to know what time it is. If you really need to know what time it actually is, you have to have a standard. There are lots of reasons for an exact measurement of time to be kept. A simple example is to be able to turn on your TV at 6 o'clock and have all the programs start at the same time. But there are other needs for exact time. Precise navigation and satellite tracking among them. Anyway, exact time is important for somebody to keep or else we would all be late, all the time.

Where do you suppose the signal for all the clocks, all around the world comes from? Would you believe Fort Collins, Colorado?

Have you ever noticed all those radio towers north of Fort Collins? That's WWV radio and the twelve towers broadcast the correct time for the entire world. The National Bureau of Standards operates WWV. The actual clock is called the Atomic Time Scale and it's in Boulder. It's based on cesium disintegration and is accurate to less than a millionth of a second.

*BIG TIME RADIO. Literally. The National Bureau of Standards built the national time station in Fort Collins in 1967. (Courtesy Style Magazine)*

In 1967, the National Bureau of Standards decided they needed a more central location to broadcast their time signals. So they looked around and chose the land between here and Wellington. They picked that location because land was cheap, and also because the soil in the area had a very high alkali content. That's lousy for growing crops, but perfect for transmitting a radio signal of the high electrical conductivity.

The building that holds the transmitters for the towers is in a depression in the terrain so that the building will not cast a shadow over the antenna patterns. The result is a crystal clear signal that goes forever.

WWV broadcasts what's called "Coordinated Universal Time." The signals are broadcast at powers up to 10,000 watts on six short wave bands. The station just ticks away the time, second by second. On the minute, they have a little celebration to give the exact time. Every hour they have a big celebration to give the exact time. The station also broadcasts information about sunspots, hurricanes, and earthquakes.

The station was put on the air in 1967 after incurring a construction cost of about a million dollars. Fort Collins Mayor Tom Bennett and Senator Gordon Allott were on hand for the ceremony.

Anybody can hear the station of short wave. The signal is very powerful. There have been reports of people who have picked it up on their toaster and one fellow said he tuned in from the fillings in his teeth.

So, when you look to the north and see the big towers, you'll know what they are. WWV is the place where time begins.

*The historic oval in the heart of Colorado State University by Lydia Dody*

W hile the rest of the country was mired in unrest and economic upheaval, Fort Collins was able to avoid most of the turbulence. The city continued to expand at record speed, and remained popular with families looking for better places to live. Fort Collins was near the top of the national list as a desirable community, perhaps because it seemed immune to the problems. It was not, however, immune from all the national issues. The Vietnam War came home at the beginning of the decade, and the environmental movement became a powerful fact, affecting every aspect of life in the Choice City.

## The 1970s At a Glance

1970   • Fort Collins population 44,000.
       • Old Main at CSU is burned to the ground by an arsonist protesting the Vietnam War.
       • Kodak opens new plant in Windsor.

1971   • DT squared is established to build civic improvements.

1973   • Foothills Fashion Mall opens.
       • The city council shelves plans for a new bypass.

1974   • Plans announced to rebuild Old Fort.

1976   • US Bicentennial is celebrated in Fort Collins.
       • Big Thompson Flood in July kills 138.

1977   • Explosion in Downtown does $1.6 million in damage.

1979   • Fort Collins rejects a limited growth initiative.

# Above the Storm

To fully appreciate Fort Collins in the decade of the 1970s, we have to understand the social and economic matrix in which it was imbedded. The United States went through the most significant upheaval and change during those ten years than any since the end of World War II. It was a tumultuous and chaotic time. The fact that Fort Collins was able to skate through the majority of the difficulties that the rest of the country faced is truly an example of a community that played by its own rules.

In the short ten years of the 1970s, the United States was:

- ripped apart by the Vietnam war
- shaken to its core by the scandal of Watergate and the first resignation of an American president in history
- swept with waves of environmental activism
- ground to a halt by an OPEC oil embargo
- crippled with double digit inflation
- mangled by unemployment
- driven into the worst economic slump since the Great Depression
- mangled by militant minorities of every kind who demanded better and more fair treatment
- faced with women demanding full equality and an Equal Rights Amendment
- contorted with people everywhere demanding self-actualization through every form of "me, first" behavior possible.

Fort Collins simply ignored about 99% of everything going on outside its borders, and went on with the business of being one of the fastest growing, most successful communities in the country. It was a remarkable achievement. The people of northern Colorado had a tendency to watch the national news every night and wonder if they were living on the same planet as the rest of the world.

In some ways, it was impossible to shut out the problems that confronted the country. Fort Collins were effected by the Vietnam War, had to get in line to buy gas, and were certainly inconvenienced by inflation and high interest rates. These were problems that the city had to work through or at least around.

Only one of the movements that swept America had a lasting effect on Fort Collins. This was the issue connected to the environmental movement. Pristine Colorado had a lot to lose by ignoring the major threats to our ecosystem, and the movement found a lot of support

SPREADING OUT. Continuous growth was making for a much larger city in area. This was easy to see because there were so few trees in the new sections. (Courtesy of John Clarke)

among the people of the state and Fort Collins. In fact, it became the seed that would grow to be the core issue of the times, twenty years later. Even as few as ten years in the future, Fort Collins would find itself choosing sides on the issues of growth and no-growth. The debate would always come down to a struggle to define a new phrase that would grow from this era: "Quality of Life." However, the central theme was generally driven by environmental considerations.

# A Landmark Dies

At the beginning of the decade, America had been involved in the fighting in Vietnam for fifteen years. It was the longest armed conflict in the nation's history. More than 1 million Americans had so far fought in the jungles of Southeast Asia, and over 30,000 had died. As Time magazine put it, "Vietnam is the wound in American life that will not heal." The war had deeply divided the country and powerful voices, from the halls of Congress to the halls of the universities were demanding that the killing stop.

But nothing would make Vietnam go away. On April 30, 1970,

**83**

President Nixon announced to a shocked country that he had ordered American ground troops into Cambodia. Since the President had told the country that he was committed to withdrawing from Vietnam and ending the war, this news came as a bombshell to most Americans. "Shorten the war by escalating it? This is madness," exclaimed Senator Edward Kennedy.

Just a few days later, tragedy struck at Kent State University in Ohio. Student activists met to protest the Cambodia invasion. That meeting was mostly peaceful, but that evening several hundred other students, threw bottles, and smashed windows in downtown Kent. The next night campus demonstrators attacked the ROTC building on campus and burned it to the ground. The National Guard was called in. Just after noon on May 4, the guardsmen moved in to break up a demonstration, rocks were thrown, tear gas was used. Moment's later shots rang out and four students lay dead, ten others were seriously wounded.

STUDENT STRIKE. Many CSU Students gathered together to decide whether they would join the hundreds of other campuses across the country in a strike to protest the Vietnam War. (Courtesy Fort Collins Public Library)

The aftermath of Kent State rang through the country. It seemed as though the unimaginable had happened. The Vietnam War had come home to America. Student strikes shut down more than 400 colleges and universities across the country.

In Fort Collins, Colorado State University was churned into a boil. All the campus was in a state of upheaval and all 15,000 students were talking about Kent State. On Friday night, May 8th, about 1,500 of those students gathered in the field house on College Avenue to "rap" about the possibility of conducting a strike at CSU. The vast majority of those present were in favor of a strike and when the vote was taken, it was overwhelmingly approved. The meeting broke

VENERABLE LANDMARK. Old Main had stood on campus since 1879. It was old, not very soundproof, and suffered from wear and tear, but everybody loved it. (Courtesy Fort Collins Public Library)

up at about 9 p.m.

An informant, who was assigned to go to the rally and attempt to buy marijuana, later said that a male student told him, "You don't have to worry about pot, something is going to burn on this campus real soon." The informant said the person was wearing a black hat, leather trousers

ABLAZE! Around 11 p.m., the first alarm was sounded. Old Main was burning. Thousands rushed to try and help, but it was too late. (Courtesy Fort Collins Public Library)

PITCHING IN. Students and townspeople worked with firemen to man the hoses and try to control the Old Main fire. Some people even came with household fire extinguishers. (Courtesy Fort Collins Public Library)

with fringe and white knee patches.

Just before 11 p.m., campus police sergeant Donald Banks called the Fort Collins Fire Department and said that he saw smoke billowing out of Old Main, the first major building built in 1879. It had served the university for nearly 90 years. It was a stately Victorian building that creaked and groaned and had such terrible acoustics that classes had to be halted every time a train came by. But, everyone loved the old building and treated it with near reverence. It had a 900-seat auditorium that was used by the entire community for theatrical productions. Now this historic landmark was burning.

Most of the Fort Collins Fire Department responded. Volunteer fire units from Timnath, Laporte, and Wellington also arrived to help. Soon the smoke from the fire erupted into huge, yellow flames that could be seen all over campus and all over Fort Collins. When the fire engines arrived, they were hampered by a "dead end" water line. This is an outlet located at the far end of a water line and has the least amount of water and pressure in that part of the system. The firemen struggled to bring another line from across West Laurel, but by this time the fire was raging completely out of control and the old building was doomed.

Hundreds of people rushed to the scene. Students, neighbors, some of them arriving in their pajamas, pitched in to try and help. Many students manned the water lines. People even brought home fire extinguishers. The prevailing emotion was one of shock, dismay and sense of loss. Large numbers of people stood behind the firelines and wept openly.

The fire burned for four hours. When the flames were finally knocked down, the building was just a burned out shell. The scarred walls were black. Five feet of debris had collapsed into a huge pile would have to be dug out before investigators could determine the cause of the fire.

Arson was suspected from the beginning. The student who was wearing the leather pants with white patches could not be positively identified by the informant and had to be released. Two other suspects were questioned and released.

The following morning was Saturday, and few classes were scheduled. Student leaders met with the press and expressed their shock and disappointment at the terrible loss. Many students wrote letters to the Fort Collins Coloradoan expressing their own feelings and saying that this act of violence did not represent the entire student body. They said that a small minority of students who had gotten out of control had caused the entire incident. A check of dormitories Saturday revealed that attendance was down 25% over the Mother's Day weekend from the previous year. Many students had left the campus.

Over 200 student marshals guarded campus buildings through the weekend against further outbreaks and expressed fear as they waited for the dawn to arrive on Monday and the resumption of classes.

When class did resume, the campus was quiet. The burning of Old Main had seemed to take the steam out of their protest. They were still upset over the war, but had never intended matters to get so disastrously out of hand. It was almost as if most of the students were embarrassed and remorseful for what had happened. Student activism continued in Fort Collins for the next several years, including a march to city hall by

JUST A SHELL. When morning came, all could see the ruins of what had been CSU's most famous building just hours before. Old Main was never rebuilt, and today is just a parking lot. (Courtesy Fort Collins Public Library)

2,000 students and faculty in September, but the violence was gone.

Following the destruction of Old Main, the cornerstone of the building was recovered from a hole in the foundation capstone. Inside the cornerstone was a "time capsule" that had been placed there when the building was dedicated. It contained a Bible, an original translation from the Greek, two Denver publications and the oldest copy of the Larimer County Express known to be in existence at that time. It was dated July 26, 1878. There were also samples of gold, silver quartz, and samples of grain and seed.

# The Malling of Fort Collins

For nearly a century, the center of commerce for Fort Collins had been downtown. As the city expanded to the south, downtown became somewhat less convenient for shoppers. Also the major chains, Penney's, Sears, and Wards, who had been located downtown from the beginning were eager to build new, larger stores with plenty of free parking. The crowded downtown was not ideal for that.

INDOOR SHOPPING. The University Mall was Fort Collins first. People liked the idea of convenient parking and shopping in heated or air-conditioned comfort, out of the weather. (Courtesy Fort Collins Public Library)

This trend was occurring in towns all over the country. As the cities grew, retail stores began locating away from the downtown centers and closer to their consumers in the suburbs. Many downtown areas simply did not survive this metamorphosis.

In Fort Collins, this trend was already well established by the beginning of the 1970s. In 1964, Mae and Bill Tiley had built their new enclosed University Mall on the south edge of town, across from their South College Heights subdivision. It was a big success, although the mall was modest by enclosed mall standards. There was just one long customer walkway. Montgomery Wards was the anchor on one end, and King Soopers was at the other end. In between, there were about two dozen stores that included the first Roley's Hallmark, the University National Bank, several clothing stores, and some specialty shops.

The next step in mall construction came just a few years later. Back on a clear day in the 1890s, you could see all the way to the river, four miles away, from the Spencer Farm. In 1968, the Everitt Company purchased the 260-acre farm. It had actually been optioned to the company clear back in 1959, when Bob Everitt and Bill Tiley had been asked to think about a location for a country club. Following the purchase of the land north of town for that purpose in 1960, those plans were scrapped.

Plans for the regional shopping center were unveiled on June 4, 1969. Everitt had entered into a joint partnership with Westcor Inc. of Phoenix, Arizona, and they proposed to build a 400,000 square foot, totally enclosed mall, with additional development around the periphery of the main center for convenience stores, banks, and theaters. The Mall would be a regional center to attract business from all over northern Colorado and southern Wyoming.

It took three more years for the planning, financing and initial leasing of space by major retailers to come into focus. Anchors Sears and

*CONSTRUCTION BEGINS. The Foothills Fashion Mall was begun in the fall of 1972. Work crews moved in and began transforming the farmland into modern shopping. (Courtesy of John Clarke)*

Denver Dry Goods had been onboard from the beginning and were instrumental in getting the project started.

Finally, on September 22, 1972, groundbreaking ceremonies were held for the new center, now named the Foothills Fashion Mall. Initial construction costs were projected at $10 million. The Mall and its parking areas would encompass 33 acres. Special traffic lights and turn lanes would have to be constructed for access off College Avenue, and other feeder roads would have to be built. It was one of the largest construction projects in Fort Collins history. A number of companies participated in the construction of the mall stores, including Reid Burton Construction Company of Fort Collins was the contractor for The Denver.

TAKING SHAPE. *The Denver Dry Goods and Sears were the first two anchor stores completed for the Foothills Fashion Mall. The grand opening was in November 1973. (Courtesy of John Clarke)*

Less than a year later, on August 9, 1973, the first two stores of the Foothills Fashion Mall opened. Sears and The Denver both conducted grand opening sales and any fears about the center being successful were wiped out in the ferocious traffic jam that resulted. Construction continued through the fall of 1973, and the grand opening of the center was in November 1973.

The mall was an immediate success. By the next year 50 stores were open, including the third anchor store, May D&F. Enclosed malls were not unknown in the area, as the city of Denver had enclosed malls in the 1960s. But such a large shopping center of climate-controlled comfort in northern Colorado was a new concept. As expected the Foothills Fashion Mall began to attract business from a wide area, beyond the city limits of Fort Collins.

# Designing Tomorrow Today

In the rush to build homes and businesses to meet the voracious appetite of a growing Fort Collins, something was lost in the process. Fort Collins had suddenly become a substantial city with close to 50,000 people in 1970. It had been less than 15,000 in 1950. In the intervening 20 years, the developers had built nearly 10,000 homes, apartments, condominiums, and townhouses. Hundreds of new businesses had been established. National chain stores and restaurants were moving to town. It was everything that a growing city with an affluent population needed. Or was it?

The infrastructure of Fort Collins had fallen well behind the development. In terms of culture, recreation, parks, sewer systems, the arts, public transportation, and libraries, the city was totally inadequate. The people were demanding better. They didn't like the idea of having to drive to Denver just to get a little live entertainment. They didn't like not having parks close to their neighborhoods. They didn't like the small library that had been built in 1904 that was smaller than some people's homes. Civic pride demanded that Fort Collins give itself some of the good things that other cities were enjoying. There was also a sense that the community did not have a clear picture of where it was heading. For the last twenty years, long range planning had meant, tomorrow.

One of the most dissatisfied persons in town was Mayor Karl Carson. He had arrived in Fort Collins in 1951 to pursue his dental practice, and had grown up with the city. He liked the excitement of growth, but felt the city needed a lot more in the way of amenities to serve the general public. He corresponded with the mayor of Indianapolis to learn about what that city was doing in the way of beautification, and he spent his own money to visit towns in Nebraska to find out about their civic improvements.

After he had gathered all this information he decided that a new public citizens group was needed

PROGRESSIVE LEADER. *Mayor Karl Carson led Fort Collins during the planning and early building of the projects of DT squared. It was his vision that gave the project life. (Courtesy Fort Collins Public Library)*

to help outline the needs for Fort Collins. He organized a committee called "Planned Development for Quality," shortened to, PDQ. The purpose of this group was to act as a citizen planning organization, with open membership, to assess the near and long term needs of the city.

On Oct 16, 1970, the PDQ Steering Committee voted to change its name to "Designing Tomorrow Today." The name was shortened to DT squared, and written either DT2 or DT². This group went right to work. In less than a month, they issued a report that projected the growth, and the needs because of that growth all the way to the year 2000. Karl Carson has since said, "Notice that we didn't go out and hire a bunch of high priced consultants to tell us what to do and take a year to do it. That never occurred to us. We just asked our own home-grown experts, and they had the answers."

The report was divided into seven parts and included projections and assessments on housing, employment, transportation, utilities, education, recreation, and social services. A priorities committee was established that organized task forces to examine each of these areas.

Every task force was open to the public. Often as many as 20 people took part. The only rules the city council set was that in order to have a vote the person had to attend a majority of the meetings. "They couldn't just show up for one or two meetings, because we didn't think that was fair," said Mayor Carson.

HARD AT WORK. Seven different task forces worked on DT squared. They looked at the total community's needs and set priorities for their completion. (Courtesy of John Clarke)

The work went on for three years. The groups met often, sometimes every week, to sift through all the needs the people said they wanted. There were some surprises. One of the issues that ended up being the number one priority for DT squared was not even on the list in the beginning. This was water, and sewer lines for Andersonville and Alta Vista. The tiny city enclaves had been on septic systems since the city was established. The priorities committee gave them the top spot on the list.

At the beginning of 1973, DT squared had completed its work. Hundreds of people had participated. The whole community had been given a place at the tables of deliberation. The final report was delivered to the city council and on January 4th, it was accepted. It was called The Master Plan of the City for Future Capital Improvements and Acquisitions.

The price tag was staggering. DT squared would cost $16 million, which was the largest capital improvements program in Fort Collins history. To put things into perspective of what this amount meant in 1973, the total budget for the entire city government that year was just $23 million. It would require a one-cent sales tax for seven years to pay for all the improvements. This was also unprecedented. That was the first sales tax to be added to the Fort Collins tax roles.

The following month, the people went to the polls and voted. They were a well-informed public due to the biggest public information campaign ever. The city council led the way. They were aided in this by the endorsements of the chamber of commerce, the newspapers and radio stations, most service clubs and public groups, and nearly all the churches. A total of 8660 votes were cast, which was the biggest turnout of voters in history. DT squared passed with overwhelming support.

What did the people approve? The list was long and varied. At the top of the list in cost was the $3 million performing arts center. For many years, people had been complaining about not having any suitable place for live performances in Fort Collins. The city had a splendid

*EXPENDABLE. The old Lincoln Junior High School, once the high school was scheduled to be torn down to make way for the new Lincoln Center. (Courtesy Fort Collins Public Library)*

symphony orchestra, led by Wil Schwartz. There were also theater groups in town, and many were looking forward to being able to attract big name entertainment from out of town. The new Lincoln Center made that all possible.

The location of the Lincoln Center was chosen because of a trade with the school district. The old Lincoln Junior High School, which was

DEMOLITION. Wrecking crews arrived in 1975 to tear down the old Lincoln Junior High building. Part of the building was saved to be used for the Lincoln Center (Courtesy Fort Collins Public Library)

UNDER CONSTRUCTION. The main performance hall at the Lincoln Center comes into shape. (Courtesy Fort Collins Public Library)

previously the high school, was past its useful life. The school district had plans to build another junior high, but the land the school sat on was a whole city block. This was plenty of room for a performing arts center and parking. Therefore, the city entered an agreement with the school district to build a new indoor swimming pool on the site and give access to it for the schools. The district donated the land. The old building was torn down. The annex, which had been built in 1953, was retained. It included the gymnasium, the library, and the auditorium. The auditorium became the mini theatre, the library became the Ludlow meeting room, the gym became the Canyon West room, and the locker room became the kitchen.

REALIZED DREAM. For years, Fort Collins had wanted a performing arts center to attend. Now it had one. In a very short time, the center was hard at work, nearly everyday of the year. (Courtesy Style Magazine)

The main performance hall rose out of the site of the old school. The eager planners of the Lincoln Center had wanted a 2,000-seat auditorium, but there was just not enough money to pay for it. The Lincoln Center Board was able to raise $350,000 to pay for improvements, but that was not enough to build a bigger theatre. In the end, they had to settle for a modest 1,172 seats. The first performance in the auditorium was held in the fall of 1978.

The second

CARNEGIE LIBRARY. Built in 1904, partly with a grant from the Carnegie Foundation, the library was one of the principal priorities of DT squared. (Courtesy Fort Collins Public Library)

largest of the DT squared projects was the new library. The old library had been built in Lincoln Park off Mathews Street, back in 1904 with a $12,500 grant from the Carnegie Foundation. It was made of red sandstone, quarried near Horsetooth Valley and too nice a building to tear down. The library board decided that the building should be used to house the Fort Collins Museum. It voted to demolish the old Pioneer Museum on the other side of the park and proposed to build the new library there.

There were problems with that location. The covenants on the property limited the size of the building that could be placed on the land. This would mean that the new library would have to be built with a smaller footprint and have the second story overhang the first to meet the requirement. This seemed like a lot of trouble for the effort. Plus, parking was strictly limited in the area.

These considerations worried the city council. They took the matter up at a meeting that went on for two and half hours before they voted, on December 4, 1974, to put the new library in Washington Park, next to the new city hall.

Public outcry was enormous. The newspaper was bombarded with letters supporting the library boards choice in Lincoln Park. The city council bowed to public pressure and agreed to let the people decide in a city referendum. Lincoln Park won easily.

BUILT ON the site of the old Pioneer Museum in Lincoln Park, the new library was an immediate success and almost as immediately proved to be too small. (Courtesy Fort Collins Public Library)

The new library cost $1.86 million. Again the funding was limited and so the library was not nearly as big as the library board had said it should be. It ended up with a total of 33,500 square feet, with 109,000 volumes, and a meeting room for 124 people. It was opened to the public on October 18, 1976.

Recreational facilities were high on the list for improvements. DT squared responded with a large new park that was named Lee Martinez Park after "Lee" Dibrado Martinez, a veteran of World War I, and remembered for his leadership within the Spanish-American community, including his support to build Holy Family Church. There was also a provision in the plan for something called the Poudre River Parkway. This is the beginning of the excellent Fort Collins trail system. Initially, the trail went along a short part of the river, near downtown, but it proved to be so popular that subsequent public improvement programs have frequently included additions to the trail system.

*THE FARM. Lee Martinez Park is unique. It houses "The Farm." A place where children can go to see farm animals and get a taste of country life. (Courtesy Style Magazine)*

Other provisions of the DT squared program included the sewers, storm drains, and sidewalks for Andersonville and Alta Vista. The city adopted a strict new sign code that prohibited all the garish signs that had crept into the landscape over the past twenty years. There was also the establishment of the Transfort bus system and Care-A-Van system to start a legitimate process of public transportation.

Finally, there was the commitment by the public through their approval of DT squared to continue the process of planning for responsible land use and growth management. It was a total effort that was embraced by a new city, filled with newcomers with hopeful hearts. As Mayor Carson said, "We have come together and done a good thing for our community and for our children. May new generations be equal to the new tasks that will face them."

# Trying to Gain Steam

By the middle of the 1970s many issues had been settled. The war in Vietnam was over and the country was again at peace. The Middle Eastern oil embargo had come and gone. There was now plenty of oil, although it now cost considerably more. However, the $8 billion Alaskan pipeline had been completed and 1.2 million barrels of oil a day were flowing into the lower 48. The travails of Watergate were passing. It's true that the country was struggling financially with double-digit inflation and high unemployment, but there was still a spirit of optimism and a certain happiness as the country began to prepare for its Bi-centennial.

Most of the problems facing the rest of the country were far less virulent in Fort Collins. The population continued to grow steadily and the economy was kept afloat because of continued construction. The Everitt

*AFFORDABLE HOUSING. The Brown Farm was the first FHA approved subdivision in Fort Collins. The average home price in the 70s was $25,000. (Courtesy of John Clarke)*

Companies were building more additions to the Parkwood area, and on the west side of town, The Brown Farm was getting into full swing. The Brown Farm was a development of John R.P. Wheeler of Greeley. He had purchased 440 acres in 1972. The development went west from Taft Hill, between Prospect and Drake. Wheeler planned 1,100 homes, his strategy was to make the subdivision the first FHA approved and financed area in Fort Collins. He was building 3 bedroom, 1,400 square foot homes, with full basements, selling for $25,000.

Dozens of small builders were developing lots and building homes in many places all across the city. Fort Collins had now grown to just under 12 square miles, or 7,500 acres.

But, inflation, price increases, and rising interest rates were a growing problem. Institutional budgets were taking a beating. The city, county, school district, hospital, and university were all scrambling to maintain an even keel in the face of such financial turbulence. Retail business was spotty.

The outlook for the downtown area was grim. In the face of increased competition from the Foothills Mall, the University Mall, many new strip centers, and the loss of the traditional anchors like Sears, Penney's and Wards, the Fort Collins downtown was facing its worst crisis in history. The problems were many, and the solutions few. The Downtown Merchants Association started working on the parking problem. Parking meters were seen as a severe handicap to customer flow. The DMA asked the city to take out the parking meters. The city refused. The DMA argued that people were not going to shop downtown and pay for parking or get tickets when they could park free and stay all day at the shopping centers. The city countered with the argument that there would be plenty of spaces to park if the employees of the businesses didn't park in front of their stores. The DMA wondered where the employees were going to park since the city did not provide any off street parking. The arguments raged on and on.

A second problem for the downtown merchants was the condition of many of the buildings. A great many of them had been built in the 19th century and were sorely in need of renovation and modernization. Since business was not very good, the store owners had a hard time keeping up with the repairs, let alone doing any significant modernization. At one

*SHOPPING IMPEDIMENT. The hated parking meters of downtown were a source of annoyance and irritation to the business owners of the area. They were finally removed. (Courtesy Fort Collins Public Library)*

meeting of the DMA in 1975, one prominent merchant suggested that all the buildings in the downtown area be torn down and a modern new shopping center be built in their place. This idea got very little support. The fact is that nobody knew what to do and the situation drifted along.

# The Bypass Gets Bypassed

General growth along the entire Front Range was producing general traffic problems for all the cities and the State of Colorado. Early in the 1970s, the Colorado Department of Transportation announced plans to build a bypass of Highway 14 from I-25 to Highway 287. The plan called for a new road that began north of Laporte and cut across the open land near the Ideal Cement Plant to the north end of College Avenue near Terry Lake. Then it would run on a diagonal from North College, along the river, to intersect with the freeway. Even then, the truck traffic was a problem for Fort Collins, as well as Laporte.

In 1972, the Fort Collins city council approved the choice of four different routes for the bypass and was making final plans with the Department of Transportation to select one of them. The cost of the new road was going to be paid for by the State of Colorado.

Then there was a city election in Fort Collins in April 1973, and new city council members were elected. They included Peggy Reeves, Chuck Bowling, and Nancy Gray. These councilpersons had questions on the bypass. In many ways, they reflected the concerns of the public.

One of the concerns was putting a major road between the main city and the subdivisions to the north, in the country club area. Chuck Bowling worried that the bypass would cut off the northern area from contact with the rest of Fort Collins. Some people were concerned about

HALF A BYPASS. The Colorado Department of Transportation built part of the highway 14 bypass, around Laporte. The rest was never built through Fort Collins, as the city squabbled over the concept. (Courtesy Style Magazine)

the property owners who would be displaced by the bypass. This was much less of an issue in 1973, than in later years because there was almost no development in the pathway of the highway. The owners of the Downtown Airpark were not very pleased to see one of the proposed routes go right through the middle of the main runway, but thought that having a major road near the airpark was an advantage.

The most serious objections to the bypass were environmental.

Part of the new road would be relatively close to the Poudre River, and part of the road would have to cross a wetland. The environmental community, led by Tom McKenna, objected to the road being built at all, because it would encourage growth adjacent to the river.

The new city council was sensitive to the issues that were brought forth and decided that the entire matter required additional study. The Department of Transportation was not sympathetic. Their position was that they had done all the work in planning the road, were willing to pay for it, and believed that all of the concerns had been met. When the City of Fort Collins proved to be unwilling to endorse the portion of the bypass that went through the city, CDOT abandoned that part of the project. They said that if Fort Collins couldn't reach a consensus on what they wanted, then they could just go about their business and Fort Collins could get back in touch when they did.

CDOT went on to build a bypass from Highway 287 just below the mouth of the Poudre Canyon and complete it to near Taft Hill Road. The city council studied the issue to death and the bypass in Fort Collins was never built.

# Let's rebuild The Fort!

With the Bi-centennial of America and the centennial of the State of Colorado just two years away, the Fort Collins Heritage Committee began sifting through suggestions on projects that fit with the themes of the state and national celebrations. An idea that came into focus was to rebuild the original "Fort" Collins. In July 1974, the Heritage commit-tee accepted Colonel Joe Mason's plan to build a replica of the old fort. They said this would be "a testimonial to our forefathers' spirit, as well as an educational vehicle for future gen-erations, by recalling the camp life of the

THE FORT. *The way it looked in 1864. Modern groups had plans to rebuild it and make it museum and tourist attraction. It never happened.*
*(Courtesy of Phil Walker)*

western armies of 1860-70." The committee gave a number of uses and benefits to building such a living museum. They felt it would be a good tourist attraction, as well as a location for local pageants and plays, displays of Western Art, and a meeting place for historical and pioneer societies.

The concept was to get the city to donate 19 acres of land between College Avenue and Linden Street and then rebuild the original fort on that land. The city owned land was the approximate site of the old city dump and was fairly close to the actual site. The committee planned to build seven buildings to include the commanding officers quarters, two officers quarters, stockade, commissary, and two company quarters. One of the enlisted quarters would serve as a museum. These buildings were planned to be faithful reproductions of the originals.

There was a lot of public enthusiasm and support for the project. Forty different local organizations and people donated over $350,000 in land, materials, and labor. The Colorado Centennial Commission gave a $10,000 grant. The city council appropriated $3,800 for a master study plan, and agreed to give up the land.

Then, somehow, the wheels started to fall off. The committee had counted on an engineering battalion of the US Army Reserves to contribute 1,000 man hours to the project in the summer of 1976, but the unit was sent to a camp in Wyoming instead. Time delays in the project made it likely that there would be cost overruns. There was a lot of concern over who would run the facility and how they would get the money to do that, year after year. In the end, the whole plan was shelved and the good idea seemed to just drift away. No serious effort to regenerate the project has ever resurfaced.

# The Big Thompson Flood

In nearly 150 years of recorded history in Colorado and Larimer County, many tragedies and events of death and destruction have been chronicled. However, the worst of these did not happen in the distant past. Instead, it was an event that occurred in the modern era, just a generation ago. It was, by far, the worst disaster to ever come to the Poudre Valley, and, indeed, all of Colorado. It was the Big Thompson Flood in 1976.

On the afternoon of July 31, 1976, a monsoonal flow of warm air brought large amounts of moisture up from the Gulf of Mexico. At the same time, a blast of cold polar air flowed in from the north. The two air masses collided over the Front Range of the Rocky Mountains, north of Denver and triggered several very slow moving thunderstorms.

The first sprinkles of rain began to fall in Fort Collins at about 5:30 PM.

During the next hour, the rain became a traditional summer cloudburst and forced a halt in the outdoors historical pageant, Larimer Legacies, that was a part of the city's Bicentennial Celebration. Participants in the performance were highly annoyed at the time, since they had worked on the pageant for weeks and had to stop right in the middle of the performance because it was raining so hard that performers and spectators alike had to run for cover.

Little did anyone know that another cell of that big storm was sitting, almost motionless over the mountains, west of Estes Park, and it was dropping a titanic amount of moisture on the upper watershed of the Big Thompson river. Beginning at about the same time as the rain in Fort Collins, the main storm stalled over the mountains and rained for four hours. A total of 12 inches, a whole foot of water fell over thousands of mountain acres. Nearly all of this water began to run downhill and had to go somewhere. Well, the somewhere was straight down the Big Thompson Canyon. On that Saturday night there were 3,000 people camped or staying in cabins in the canyon.

By 7 p.m., the water in the river inside the canyon began to rise rapidly. At 7:30 p.m. calls to the Larimer County Sheriff's office from area residents reported that, in addition to the water rising in the river, that

CHURNING MONSTER. *The Big Thompson River scoured out its canyon and took most of the road with it.* (Courtesy Fort Collins Public Library)

big rocks were falling on the highway. It was also at this time that the first warning was broadcast on the radio. The warning read, "Severe thunderstorms are possible in Eastern Larimer County until 9 p.m. Local flooding can occur in low lying areas." It was a routine broadcast, but by that time, some people in the Big Thompson Canyon were already fighting for their lives.

By 8 p.m. that night, rain was falling at the rate of five inches per hour with the storm at its peak.

At 8:25, State Patrolman Bill Miller radioed the first cries for help and warning to the police in Estes Park. He reported that the flooding was becoming widespread. "This is going to

**103**

be awful!" he said. "Now somebody up there push the red button and get everybody within 50 miles moving, and I mean right now! We have to evacuate this canyon!"

A few minutes later, Larimer County Sheriff's Deputy, Larry Wyer told his dispatcher in Fort Collins the very same thing, but more profanely.

The Big Thompson Canyon is in Larimer County, which made the Larimer County Sheriff the overall responsible agency to coordinate the actions of all the people who would be needed to react to this onrushing calamity. There was a plan to deal with a major disaster, such as a flood in the Big Thompson Canyon, and it was rapidly put into action.

Highway 34 going up the Big Thompson Canyon is a state road, and is routinely monitored by the Colorado Highway Patrol. That night the State Troopers became the point men into the disaster area. Their job

TONS OF DEBRIS. The force of the river swept everything before it, and left grim reminders of what had been in its path. (Courtesy Fort Collins Public Library)

was to get into the canyon and start taking whatever emergency actions were required to preserve lives and property, lives being the main priority.

At 8:44 p.m., law enforcement agencies began networking with one another to establish that the emergency existed and that immediate steps were needed. The first priority was to warn everyone in the canyon and evacuate all 3,000 of them before the entire canyon filled up with water and drowned everyone of them!

In Loveland, State Patrolman Hugh Purdy heard all the traffic on his police scanner in his home. He immediately went out and got into his patrol car and took off up the canyon. It was raining so hard that he could barely see to drive, but he was trying to go so fast that he was nearly killed at every turn he took as he drove the jagged narrows just inside the canyon. The river was a raging torrent and rose rapidly toward the road! Patrolman Purdy struggled on into the curtains of water that fell out of the black night.

At 9 p.m., Denver radio warned "that thunderstorms are moving slowly north along the Front Range and that local flooding could occur." In the Big Thompson Canyon it was raining so hard you couldn't see your hand in front of your face, and people were beginning to die.

At 9:15 p.m., Sheriff's Deputies Terry Urista and Jim Garcia radioed to the dispatcher in Fort Collins. They said that they were at Cedar Grove and that everyone should get out of the canyon and away from the river....NOW! The two deputies barely escaped with their lives and were trapped just above the river for two days.

At that same moment, Patrolman Purdy radioed that he was in trouble. "I can't get out! I'm right in the middle of it!" Then he told the dispatcher the canyon had to be evacuated. Then his radio went dead.

Between 9:30 and 10 p.m., the harried dispatchers of all the emergency agencies stepped up their efforts to get every available unit into the canyon and warn everyone to evacuate. A roadblock was set up at the mouth of the canyon to keep people from going in. Some people had just come to see for themselves and actually thought they could drive up the canyon and look at the big flood in the river. Others were trying to get to members of their family who were

*TOSSED LIKE MATCHSTICKS. Whole homes were washed away, and swept down the river to crash against anything that lay in the way. (Courtesy Fort Collins Public Library)*

already in the canyon. The sheriff turned everyone away.  The priority was to get everyone out.  A solid line of cars where rolling out of the canyon and there was no mistaking the terror on the faces of the people as they drove by.

At 10:30 p.m., the rain began to let up.  There was not a single person in the entire area that was fooled by that.  The people knew that the worst was yet to come.  The crest of the flood still lay many miles to the west near the top of the canyon.

Sure enough.  Between 10:30 and 11 p.m., a wall of water nearly 20 feet tall came washing down the canyon.  Billions of gallons of water, roaring in a fury beyond description, and was sweeping up cars, houses, businesses, trees, boulders and....people.

At 11 p.m., when the crest of the flood reached the Dam Store at the mouth of the canyon, debris began to smash into the massive supports for the enormous water siphon pipe that stretched across the road.  An entire house, swept along by the flood, rammed the biggest concrete support and reduced it to gravel.  The siphon collapsed onto the road.  Nobody was going in or out of the canyon now.  Filled with water, as it was, the pipe weighed over a million pounds.

Also at that time, the National Weather service issued its first flash flood warning of the night.  It said, "A Flash Flood Warning is in

HUMAN SCALE.  There were 3,000 people in the Big Thompson Canyon on the night of the flood.  They abandoned their cars and ran for their lives. (Courtesy Fort Collins Public Library)

effect until 4 a.m. for persons near the Big Thompson River from Loveland to Greeley. A Flash Flood Warning means that flooding is imminent. Take necessary precautions as required." To all of the people nearby, the flooding was a good deal more than just imminent!

At that moment, the water at the mouth of the canyon was measured at 19 feet above the normal level of the river. The Big Thompson would normally flow at about 165 cubic feet per second. Now the flow was over 31,000 cubic feet per second. That's 233,000 gallons of water per second.

When the sun came up, deputies, patrolmen, mother and fathers, sons and daughters, made their back into the Big Thompson Canyon. The destruction was beyond belief. As rescue helicopters flew along the route of the canyon, the pilots reported that everything in the canyon had been laid waste. Much of the road had completely disappeared. The river had gouged new channels and changed course many times. Everywhere there was mud and debris, and cars were littered by the hundreds along the canyon floor.

The pilots also reported that they could see many bodies buried in the mud and smashed like rag dolls. Many hundreds more were clinging to precarious safety along the slopes of the canyon, waving at the helicopters to save them. The rescue operations kept the emergency crews and helicopters busy all day long. Every person who survived that ordeal had stories of terror and agony to tell. All of them repeated, many times, that they were just grateful to be alive.

The entire State of Colorado mobilized to give aid to the people of Larimer County in this most destructive natural disaster in the history of the state. Governor Dick Lamm said, "The river had reclaimed the canyon from all its intruders."

The gruesome job of recovering and identifying all the bodies went on for days. Among the first of the bodies recovered was that of State Patrolman Hugh Purdy, who was found downstream, many miles from his last known location. In the end, the death count was between 139 and 150 people. Some bodies were never recovered, and some were never identified.

When the total damage was assessed, in addition to the death toll, the river had destroyed over 600 homes and businesses and the flood damage amounted to over 56 million dollars. It took two years to rebuild the road and over ten years for the canyon to return to normal.

It has been called a "thousand year flood," but that doesn't mean that it couldn't happen again tomorrow.

# Explosion Rocks Downtown Fort Collins

It was cold overnight on April 26, 1977. Spring was late that year. A blustery sky shrouded the stars. The furnaces in the buildings of downtown Fort Collins were humming, as warm air was needed to heat the stores, offices, and shops. All save one. In the basement of the Robertson Building at the corner of College and Oak, there was only the sound of hissing as natural gas drifted into the air from a cracked pipe.

The gas had been leaking for hours. It filled the basement and seeped up the stairs into the main building that housed a number of businesses. During the day, store workers and customers would have detected the smell of gas almost immediately, but in the dark hours of night, there was no one to sound the alarm.

By dawn, the smell of gas was so strong, it was noticed by two early morning workers in the Elks Lodge across the alley on Oak Street. Sam Schmidt searched the building, but found nothing. Still the odor of gas was unmistakable. It had to be coming from somewhere close by. The two men wondered what they should do.

At 7:26 a.m., a tiny spark from a forever unknown source, flared.

LIKE A WAR ZONE. The downtown explosion made kindling of buildings. Most of the Robertson Building and part of the Elks Lodge were destroyed. (Courtesy Fort Collins Coloradoan)

The pent-up gas exploded with the fury of a bomb. The shock wave of the explosion rolled through Fort Collins and was heard and felt six miles away. Residents as far south as Trilby Road, and as far north as Wellington heard the blast.

At the center of the explosion, the entire rear of the Robertson Building vaporized instantly. Most of the building just ceased to exist. Tons of debris, paper, wood, glass, and stone were hurled 85 feet into the air. In the Elks Lodge, the two workers were knocked off their feet. They scrambled to a door and found it jammed. They climbed through a broken window as debris began falling all around them.

For four blocks in all directions the explosion shattered plate glass windows, damaged storefronts, blew open doors, and rattled buildings, causing structural damage. In private homes a quarter of a mile away, windows were smashed and screens were blown out of their frames. Across the street at the Cinema 35 theatre the tremor turned on three popcorn machines that promptly began spewing out popcorn, and all the soft drift spigots jammed in the on position.

The Fort Collins police quickly cordoned off the area from the thousands of spectators who had gathered to stand in wonder at the destruction. Oak, Remington, and College Avenues were closed. Officers patrolled the area to prevent looting. The bomb squad and the fire department began to sift through the rubble in search of the cause. Damage control experts allowed business owners back into their stores on College Avenue the next day, following an inspection of the entire block.

Four businesses: Hickman's For Men, Bowen's Book Store, Flowers and Things, and the Mesa Insurance Company were completely destroyed. Dozens of other businesses and offices reported damage.

The Elks Lodge had actually planned to remodel their building prior to the explosion. After the blast, the members learned that the rear of the building had been so badly damaged that; it would have to be torn down. Renovation and repairs took over a year and half and cost $1.2 million.

There were no injuries in the explosion because it had occurred before the start of the business day. If it had happened even a half hour later, there would have been extensive loss of life.

In the aftermath of the explosion, the costs were placed at $1.6 million. Four insurance companies filed civil damage suits against Public Service Company for negligence in delivering gas. In 1980, a jury acquitted Public Service Company saying that they did not believe there was any negligence on their part. No definitive cause for the explosion was ever determined.

# Enter the Dreamer

A great city deserves to have great dreamers. True visionaries that stand above their peers, and who mold and shape the world about them into a new and realities that alter and illuminate the lives of everyone. Fort Collins has had several such men.

One such man is Gene Mitchell, philosopher, reflective thinker, theorist, sage, wise person, and logician. Each of these qualities were necessary for Mitchell to produce his astonishing list of achievements in Fort Collins.

Mitchell spent his childhood in upstate New York. He attended Hartwick College in New York, transferred to Ohio State, transferred again to Northwestern, and completed law school at the University of Kansas. After graduation in 1952, he joined his father-in-law's practice in Wichita.

By 1955, Gene had come to believe that relationships in a large law firm were too impersonal. He needed more personal and professional freedom. His wife loved Colorado. They set established criteria for a new hometown, amenities, potential, and progressive attitudes, resulting in them choosing Fort Collins.

"I HAVE A DREAM!" Gene Mitchell built all over Fort Collins, but his heart was always downtown. (Courtesy The Mitchell Company)

Mitchell joined the law firm of Allen, Mitchell, Rogers, and Metcalf, where he became a partner. The young lawyer, who worked overtime and chose causes, brought his ethical sensitivity to Fort Collins with him. When his law partner, Bill Allen, resigned from the Poudre School Board in 1966, Mitchell was appointed to fill out his term, and went on to run for three elections of his own. Altogether, he spent ten years on the school board and instituted a program called the "Fair Share" plan. As Mitchell remembers, the Fair Share plan provided an opportunity for all those working in the Poudre R-1 school district to sit down and ask, "What are we trying to do?" The components of the system, education, transportation, administration, and so forth, were rated as to their importance, and a percentage of the funds were assigned to the function.

"This took away the adversary approach of opponents fighting for their share of the funds, to one based on trust and cooperation," said Mitchell.

When Mitchell resigned from the board in 1976, there was a standing ovation for him, the negotiating teams, and for the "Fair Share Plan."

Mitchell's business interests were growing at the same time he was serving on the school board. In 1963, he joined with Gary Johnson, a mechanical engineer, in Heath Engineering Company. In 1968, Mitchell and Johnson acquired control of the company. That year it had done $110,000 in volume of business. Ten years later Heath Engineering was doing $8 million in volume.

Mitchell and Johnson remained close friends throughout the years. Johnson referred to Mitchell as, "my not so silent partner, my hyperactive counselor."

In 1972, Mitchell's career took off in a new direction. His long time friend and associate, John Strachan, was working with the dilemma of what to do with the remaining parcels of land left unsold from his sprawling south-side farm. He had sold so much land that it was not profitable to raise any crops. Ultimately he reorganized his previous farm operations into a land corporation and merged it with the Mitchell Company.

The land from the Strachan farm was the 120 acres that ran along Drake from Stover to Lemay. Mitchell, in cooperation with Melvin Johnson, worked to design a new kind of neighborhood for this parcel. It was a unique concept, unprecedented in Fort Collins, and mostly unheard of in modern suburbia.

The development was called Scotch Pines. It was the first mixed residential, totally planned community in Fort Collins. It featured better design accents. It was somewhat similar to Fairway Estates nearly 20 years before, the park area, the greenbelts, and the open spaces were designed to compliment the building lots. The subdivision was mixed use from the beginning with apartments, patio homes and nearby single family residences all clustered together in a park-like setting. All the homes and buildings were upscale with shake shingle roofs, brick fronts and solid wood construction. It was a showcase subdivision that fit Mitchell's concept of what should be built in Fort Collins. "We always strove to make a statement," he said. "We wanted to build things that did something for the town. We go for the high road, the top end."

**111**

*UPSCALE LIVING. Scotch Pines was designed as more than just apartments or patio homes. The subdivision had many amenities built into a park like atmosphere. (Courtesy The Mitchell Company)*

*TRENDY SHOPPING. The Scotch Pines Village at the corner of Drake and Lemay was built "California Style" with a low profile and high quality. (Courtesy The Mitchell Company)*

At the corner of Lemay and Drake, Mitchell built Scotch Pines Village. It was the commercial center for the neighborhood with "California Style" low profile upscale styled development. The anchor for the center was Toddy's Supermarket, a leader in the grocery business. Scotch Pines

Village was compatible with the rest of the neighborhood. The whole complex was nestled back from the corner with the parking area hidden in the middle of the center. The city administration considered the entire Scotch Pines development to be the prototype for quality future building in Fort Collins, and asked builders to model their construction after what Mitchell had built. The project was completed in 1979.

At the same time that Scotch Pines was being developed, Mitchell was moving ahead with a much more ambitious commercial project. By 1976, he had assembled partners to acquire the land from the Foothills Mall, south to Horsetooth Road, and from College Avenue to Stanford St., this area came to be known as the Arena property.

Mitchell believed that the best commercial retailing site in Larimer County was at the intersection of Horsetooth and College and would be the center of Fort Collins merchandising for the future.

His newest dream was for an intimate, European styled, shopping center with convenience and style. The 120,000 square foot shopping center would be called The Square. His original idea was to offer a clear central span with small shops standing free. The perimeter of the building would house the larger anchor stores.

For the anchors of The Square, Mitchell achieved a marketing coup. He was able to convince the very prestigious Neusteters Company to locate a store in Fort Collins. In later years, after Neusteters closed all their stores, he attracted Fashion Bar. Mitchell's friends just shook their heads and said, "He did it again!"

The Square would be a controlled environment, which would result in a 25% saving in energy over the more common plan where each store

DESIGNED TO BE DIFFERENT. *The Square was a different kind of shopping center. Originally, Mitchell wanted a wide-open central area with stores around the perimeter. (Courtesy The Mitchell Company)*

**113**

controlled their own thermostat. It cost more money initially. The new center had a healthy construction price tag of $7 million. It was completed and opened in the fall of 1978.

Quickly, Mitchell built other retail businesses around The Square, and soon the corner of Horsetooth and College hummed with activity, just as he had predicted.

It was only the beginning. The biggest of the Mitchell projects were yet to come in the next decade.

## The End of the Decade Brings Philosophical Changes

As early as the middle of the 1970s, a new activism was developing in Colorado. Powerful voices were being raised in opposition to the whole concept of growth. Led by environmental organizations, and supported by a considerable fraction of the population, growth, the effects of growth, the loss of open spaces, increased traffic and pollution and sprawling housing developments were put on the political front burners.

It was an unbelievably complicated issue to confront. Colorado was enjoying a better economy than most of the country because migration into the state was producing many new jobs in industry, commerce, construction, and education. But the very existence of all this expansion was producing a negative effect on the pristine vistas and environment of the state. One of the largest industries in the state was tourism. The whole world seemed to want to vacation in Colorado because of its natural wonders and beautiful mountains. Natives and newcomers alike were very protective and proprietary about preserving these gifts of nature, and the preeminence of the environmental ethic struck a responsive cord in the hearts of Colorado residents.

The first sign that the environmental movement was going to seriously affect public policy in Colorado was the open opposition by Democratic Governor Dick Lamm, to the awarding of the Winter Olympics to Colorado. Lamm led the effort to force a statewide referendum of the games. This was done after the International Olympic Committee had given Denver the endorsement. Lamm argued that the Olympic Games would produce an environmental disaster for Colorado. He was also certain that the Olympic Games would be a financial quagmire from which Colorado would take years to recover. The Colorado Olympic Committee at first scoffed at the opposition, and then, in a panic, began a huge public relations campaign to convince the voters that the Olympics represented a tremendous opportunity for Colorado.

114

They presented reams of statistics that showed how the environmental damage would be slight and temporary, but it was too late. The voters rejected the games, and they were moved to Lake Placid, New York in 1980, where the U.S. hockey team shocked the world, and electrified America with their Gold medal over the Russians.

Encouraged by their victory, serious no growth supporters, limited growth and isolationist groups began campaigns to permanently effect the growth philosophy of Colorado. Boulder was the most outspoken community in the state, and in the same year the Olympics were rejected, the people of Boulder voted to limit annual growth in the city to 2%. They also enacted what came to be known as the "Blue Line," which ringed Boulder with open space, and effectively isolated and constrained the city within the line.

Similar movements were begun in other Front Range cities. Fort Collins was one of them. In 1979, a voter referendum patterned after Boulder's was introduced in the Choice City. A heated debate ensued. The people of Fort Collins now had a model to view. Opponents to the referendum pointed out that real estate prices in Boulder had begun to skyrocket because of the limited supply of new homes being built. They pointed out that economic activity in Boulder had slowed significantly and that the tax base of the city was eroding. Those in favor of the proposition discounted the effects of the limited growth initiative in Boulder and pointed out that growth in the surrounding areas of Boulder County was booming. The smaller towns near Boulder were growing faster than any other place in Colorado. New jobs were being created at a fantastic rate. Opponents in Fort Collins agreed this was true, but that the effect was mindless sprawl that was causing people to drive farther to commute to jobs thereby creating more pollution, and that this was the very thing that the growth limitation had sought to stop.

When Fort Collins voted on the growth initiative, it was defeated overwhelmingly. However, a new mindset had emerged from the debate, which caused the people of the city to be much more sensitive to the idea of managed growth and more careful planning. The environmental movement had scored a significant victory in Fort Collins because they had gained many new supporters to the concepts of open space, limited construction on the foothills west of Fort Collins, and an emerging willingness on the part of the city administration to take a more active role in the manner in which development could occur.

With these new factors now absorbed into the social, economic and political scene, Fort Collins roared into the next decade.

*The restored Poudre Valley Bank in Old Town Square by Lydia Dody*

F ort Collins had grown to over 65,000 people.  That made it one of the fastest growing cities in America, and it attracted a lot of attention.  National companies were targeting Fort Collins for future expansion.  Hewlett-Packard, NCR, Kodak, and Woodward Governor were all firmly established and expanding.  Fort Collins was also targeted in another way.  A very vocal segment of the population was concerned about this growth.  They viewed it as being destructive rather than an economic bonanza.  This group, led by environmental concerns, was determined to staunch the flow and put real limits on the amount and type of growth.  It was a battleground that made the people of Fort Collins choose sides.  The vast majority of the people had moderate views that allowed them to see both sides of the issue.  In a spirit of fairness, they swung their support back and forth on a case by case basis.

## The 1980s At A Glance

1980 • Fort Collins population is 64,236.

• Money Magazine declares Fort Collins one of the ten best cities in America.

1981 • Downtown Development Association is approved by voters.

1982 • Drake Crossing Shopping Center is built near Brown Farm.

1983 • City Councils approves historic trolley to run on Mountain Avenue.

1984 • Highest winds in history.  95 mile per hour wind causes $1 million in damage.  Winds at Rawhide Power Plant clocked at 145 miles per hour.

1985 • Old Town Square is opened.   Fort Collins Marriott opens for business.
• University Park Holiday Inn is completed.
• Thomas Sutherland is kidnapped and held hostage in Lebanon.

1987 • Budweiser Brewery opens.

# How Busy Was My Valley

The opening of the decade of the 80s found Fort Collins churning with activity. The people didn't need national polls and magazines to tell them their Community was one of the fastest growing cities in America. They could see it, feel it, and experience it on all fronts, everyday. Many groups, from government to private enterprise were laboring

*WITHOUT A PAUSE, Fort Collins continued to grow. The city was chosen by Money Magazine as one of the top cities in America in which to live. (Courtesy of John Clarke)*

to handle all the issues confronting them. City planning was a major subject. Because the city was growing so rapidly, unincorporated border areas along the city limits were a problem. These areas were often developed without the same standards as the city and when they were brought into the city limits, they were, to say the least, non standard to city specifications. For example, it was easy to build a subdivision like Fairway Estates in the 1960s, when it was miles away from the city limits. But by 1980, Harmony Road was targeted for annexation and none of the streets, water systems, or curbs and gutters were up to city code in the subdivision. It was a difficult problem. Do you annex the subdivision and spend city funds to bring the infrastructure up to code? Do you assess the property owners in the subdivision to pay for the improvements? Or do you ignore the subdivision and let it become a tiny, county enclave within the city limits? This sort of problem was occurring throughout the City of Fort Collins.

The city addressed this problem in 1980 with the Urban Growth Area Plan. Essentially, the plan looked at areas surrounding the city limits that would be annexed at some time in the future. An intergovernmental agreement was signed with Larimer County that established guidelines for development within the boundary. The plan also developed regulations for zoning. This went a long way to insure that future annexations would be more in keeping with the city standards, which were much

ANNEXING SUBDIVISIONS, like Fairway Estates, into the city was a problem when the subdivision didn't meet the city codes. There were many such non-standard areas. (Courtesy Style Magazine)

stricter than the county's standards.

Next, the city faced the matter of efficient development within the city limits, and, in 1981, developed the Land Development Guidance System. This award-winning plan provided for commercial and service centers to be evenly distributed throughout the community. The population density, meaning the number of homes and apartments you could build in a subdivision, was based on the developer's land acquisitions for shopping centers, parks, access to transit routes, employment centers, day care facilities, schools, and parking. The more of these features that were included in the development, the more households could be constructed. It was based on a point system. It was a very good system. For the developers, there was a certain predictability in their planning. For the city, it was advantageous to build well-planned neighborhoods that would limit driving and consequently pollution. As a result, the homeowners got convenience and an array of amenities that made living in the new area a plus. The one thing the plan didn't do was to limit growth in general. Fort Collins continued to expand explosively.

# The Downtown Development Authority

The redevelopment and renovation of downtown Fort Collins had been on the drawing boards since the mid 1970s when Foothills Mall, The Square and other strip centers started taking business away from the historic downtown district. There was never a single thought to abandoning downtown, or letting it deteriorate into a slum. Rather,

LOVELY TO LOOK AT, but expensive to hold. The many historic downtown buildings were in need of renovation and repair. The Downtown Development Authority was created to help. (Courtesy of John Clarke)

people had more lofty goals in mind for downtown. This was an easy choice. Many western cities, built in the 1880s, had been poorly constructed, badly planned, and made out of wood. As the years went by, the value of these building, both financially and esoterically, went down dramatically. But, Fort Collins was different. Most of the primary buildings downtown had been built solidly with high quality, native sandstone, quarried just a few miles from the city. They were well designed and their builders had intended them to last. Last, they had, right up to the 1980s when their character became their greatest asset.

The city council had directed the staff to formulate plans for improving the downtown area. Many businessmen had participated in the process, and the Downtown Merchants Association was active in helping to encourage the process. A new entity, called the Downtown Development Authority, was created, and presented to the voters for approval in March 1981. Upon voter approval, the DDA was in business. Basically, it was a new tax district, a public non-profit agency. The DDA board was made up of property owners, and one member of the city council. The DDA provided financial incentives for developers to build downtown, because it was more expensive to build there. Scarce land and the presence of existing buildings that could not be torn down due to their historic designation made renovation and building costly. Furthermore, the decay of the downtown area made it less attractive to businesses and developers. Financial incentives provided by DDA helped bridge the gap.

Funding for the DDA came from a new 5-mil tax levy on buildings located within the DDA boundaries. A bigger incentive was tax increment funding. That referred to any increase in taxes on a downtown property as a result of the property being improved and having a higher appraised value, could be retained by the district for new development

*MORE PARKING. One of the first projects of the DDA was to build a new parking structure. It helped to alleviate the off-street parking problem. (Courtesy Style Magazine)*

and new improvements. This was a powerful incentive and soon business owners and developers were taking advantage of it.

Among the first projects built by the DDA was the new parking garage at the corner of Mountain and Remington. This facility was a key element in providing off street parking for shoppers as well as employees downtown. New housing and street development followed, and from evolved plans for the development of a new downtown hotel and convention center. The DDA was very interested in creating a better atmosphere for shopping downtown. Soon, they were to get the biggest boost to the area of them all - Old Town Square.

# Old Town Square

Gene Mitchell had a dream. All through the years he spent building up his company, developing real estate in south Fort Collins, and putting himself on solid financial footing, he had a dream. His vision was focused on downtown Fort Collins in general and Old Town specifically.

When Mitchell looked at a map of Fort Collins, he saw a geographical anomaly. In the days before Franklin Avery platted the town in 1873, an older version of city plat had been drawn. This one was laid out with streets oriented to the river. Avery kept that original idea, but laid out all the rest of his Fort Collins along compass lines. This meant that the original streets were at a 45-degree angle from the new streets. They formed a triangle that used the river as a base and narrowed down to the point of the triangle that met at Mountain Avenue. The central street was Linden. It ran all the way to the river. In actuality there are ten full city blocks, and parts of six more city blocks broken into smaller triangles, that form the main triangle that is known as Old Town.

The term Old Town, was used first to distinguish those businesses in the triangle from the businesses that moved to College Avenue and Mountain Avenue. This was called New Town. There was a tremendous rivalry between merchants in the two sections that raged for years before New Town won the economic battle. Thereafter, Old Town was relegated to second class stores and a generally depressed economic environment. It was in sorry shape by the time merchants, and city officials began talking about doing something to renovate the area in the mid 1970s.

One of the local radio stations, KTCL, began a sales campaign to improve the image of the area. Deni LaRue remembers that in all their commercials they would promote coming to "Old Town," a term that had been out of favor for most of a hundred years. One local bar owner liked the term so much he changed the name of his bar to; "Sam's Old Town Bar." The business was in the entire Miller Block at the corner of Linden and Walnut Street.

Putting a nostalgic name on the area did little to improve its blighted character. What was needed was an entirely new approach. A breath of fresh air arrived on the gilded tongue of Gene Mitchell in 1980.

Yes, Gene Mitchell had a dream. He looked at the triangle and won-

HARD TIMES. By 1980, Linden Street was no longer a commercial center. The charm of the great old buildings was buried under the squalor of an Old Town that was deteriorating. (Courtesy Fort Collins Public Library)

dered if the entire area, from the river, all the way to the south end of Linden Street couldn't be entirely redeveloped. The scope of the project was enormous, the problems were unending, and the price was staggering. Mitchell could see that his dream was almost impossible to realize. That being the case, he did it anyway.

Mitchell had always wanted to work the downtown area. His heart was always downtown. His projects in the south were important, but really only tune-ups for the main event he was about to begin.

One of the main partners at Mitchell and Company was young Dave Sitzman. He was a CPA by training. It was his adroit money management that would guide the Mitchell Company through all of the roadblocks that lay in the pathway of the Old Town project. In fact, he was opposed to the project because he thought it was risky and didn't make good economic sense. But Mitchell would say, "A town is judged by its downtown." The project was started.

Mitchell's idea was to redevelop the entire triangle. He would use the river as a base and reattach it to the main part of the city. He reasoned that the river and the land next to it, all the way south to Jefferson Street, had been cut off shortly following the founding of the town in 1873. Jefferson Street itself had been a barrier, and when the Union Pacific Railroad put in tracks along Jefferson Street in 1909, that finished the job.

The site of the original Fort was still undeveloped, the land close to the river had been used as the city dump for many years, and the construction that was near the river was modest indeed. Mitchell's plan was

THE EVE OF RENAISSANCE. This was Old Town on the night before the construction crews arrived to begin creating Old Town Square. (Courtesy Fort Collins Public Library)

to redevelop that land with parks, pathways, and restaurants, maybe even rebuild a replica of the fort. He thought the land would be a great place for an outdoor amphitheater for entertainment, and saw a time when people would be able to stroll along the river and enjoy all sorts of diversions and recreation.

Mitchell didn't have a slash and burn mentality toward all the historic buildings in the Old Town area. Quite the contrary. He saw the buildings as beautiful and worth restoring and saving. It was true that over the years, some of the original buildings had been torn down, or burned or remodeled into obscurity, but most of them were intact and would serve as a perfect setting to let the turn of the century style of Fort Collins return everyone to a quieter, more serene atmosphere.

His plan was to turn the two blocks of Linden from Mountain to Jefferson and the two blocks of Walnut between College and Mountain into a vast plaza. It would be a pedestrian center with fountains and pocket parks and all the buildings restored to their original forms.

Somewhere in the plan, he hoped to be able to restore the trolley to serve as fun, convenient mass transit for the entire area. He saw the trolley making a loop along the river, up Linden, over to College and back to the river. It would be a ring around the entire Old Town area.

THE BEST OF THE PAST. Construction to make Old Town Square come alive concentrated on preserving and beautifying the entire area with style and charm. (Courtesy Fort Collins Public Library)

With this vision firmly in his mind, Mitchell embarked on the grand plan.

From 1980 to 1983, the goal of Mitchell and Company was to buy every building in Old Town. The company very nearly did it. Certainly, the vast majority of the buildings on both sides of Linden Street came into the Mitchell camp. A major disappointment in the process was the Avery Building that sprawls on the corner of College, Mountain and Linden. It's one of the most famous of the Old Town buildings, and one that was the most in need of maintenance. The owner, Paul Wagner, wouldn't even return Mitchell's calls, and he had to work around the building throughout the renovation process. However, most of the rest of the land and buildings on Linden Street became Mitchell property.

Early on, it was obvious that the mouth of Old Town Square at the corner of Linden and Mountain was going to need a new building. Mitchell designed one that would be compatible to the other buildings on the street. It was larger than the others were, and he was criticized for that, but then he was generally criticized and scoffed at a lot. Regardless, Mitchell just went single-mindedly on his way.

In 1984, Mitchell founded the Poudre River Trust. It was a non-profit organization formed to promote revitalization along the Cache la Poudre River. Mitchell intended the trust to derive its power from the cooperation, enthusiasm, and dedication of people interested in improving the riverfront area. The organization continues today with the same outlook and is supported by private property owners, special interest groups, public entities, developers, and other interested citizens of Fort Collins.

The work in Old Town went on for nearly five years. Linden Street, between Mountain and Walnut was vacated by the

INSTANT ATTRACTION. That's what Old Town Square was for the people of Fort Collins. It captured their imagination, and they came often. (Courtesy The Mitchell Company)

city to allow Mitchell to turn it into a plaza.  Financial woes plagued the project from the beginning.  A dispute with a major partner, Madsen Company of Madison, Wisconsin, caused many delays.  Old Town Square was supposed to open in 1984, but was not completed until mid 1985.  The delays caused the project's costs to skyrocket.  During that time other retail and office buildings were built throughout the city and some of the opportunities Mitchell had to attract tenants were lost.  By the time Old Town had its grand opening, Mitchell had invested $20 million.

By 1988, the pressure on the Mitchell Company for Old Town Square and for his equally large commercial project in the building of the Marriott Hotel, plus the fact that the general economic climate of the Country was terrible, caused the system to collapse.  Mitchell's principal money source, Continental Casualty, foreclosed on his loan and force him to give up many of his Fort Collins holdings, including Old Town Square.

Mitchell was amazingly upbeat about it all.  "There's great strength in being willing to go broke," he said.  He was equally upbeat about his achievement with Old Town.  "It's there and it will put a stamp down-town that will never be removed.  You can already see that's where the people go."

Today, it's hard to imagine a Fort Collins without an Old Town Square.  It is consistently rated as the number one gathering spot in Fort Collins.  Whenever visitors come to Fort Collins, they usually make a point of seeing Old Town!  It is a source of pride and accom-plishment for the entire city, which has embraced the center and taken ownership of it.

The only regret Gene Mitchell has is that he was able to finish only about 10% of his dream.  "If we would have gotten all of it built, it would have been the wonder of America and our economic outlook through tourism would be dramatically different."  He is unquestionably right.

# Too much at the Wrong Time

In the middle of these troubled economic times two large hotels were built in Fort Collins.  There was only supposed to be one, and it was supposed to be built downtown.  The Mitchell Company had opened a dialogue with John Hammons, the developer, and owner of a number of Holiday Inns in this region.  Difficulties, delays, and dispute developed almost immediately.  Mitchell grew more and more suspicious of Hammons' motives and came to believe that he was only interested in getting  the insight into how to work with the city in preparation for his

*BEAUTIFUL NEW HOTELS. Both the University Park Holiday Inn and the Marriott, (shown here) were prestigious additions to Fort Collins. But the total of the two exceeded the demand for room space. (Courtesy Style Magazine)*

own project. Mitchell abandoned the relationship in 1983. Hammons went on to build the University Park Holiday Inn on Prospect Street, saying that he was building a convenient facility, close to CSU. Over the objections of the neighbors, the city council approved construction of the Holiday Inn on a 4 to 3 vote.

Mitchell was undaunted by the Holiday Inn and was able to enlist the Marriott Corporation on the idea of building a hotel close to The Square at the intersection of College and Horsetooth. He began construction in 1984, and opened the hotel in 1985. It cost $16 million to build.

The sudden arrival of 500, high-priced hotel rooms in Fort Collins made it difficult for either of the hotels to be profitable and it was several years before the demand caught up with the supply.

Meanwhile, Mitchell was faced with more trouble in his Old Town project with delays and disputes with his financial partners. The result was that the economy, circumstances, and competition nearly broke his company.

# This Bud's for Us

In 1981, the giant Anheuser-Busch Corporation of St. Louis, Missouri, began looking for a new site to build a brewery. They settled on Colorado as the best geographical site. Soon development teams were moving through the state. Budweiser settled on three possible locations; Pueblo, Greeley, and Fort Collins. They wooed those communities. Pueblo was the most eager to accommodate the company. They offered free land, free water, and tax incentives. Busch just didn't like Pueblo.

127

*EASILY RECOGNIZED. The Anheuser-Busch logo is well known. When the company began looking for a location for a new brewery, Fort Collins was in the thick of the hunt. (Courtesy Style Magazine)*

They felt their employees would not be happy in that town. Greeley made their best offer of free land, no water, and no mineral rights on the land. Busch balked at that provision. They felt they ought to own the mineral rights on any land they owned. Fort Collins had the worst offer. It demanded Busch buy the land, buy the water, and would only negotiate any tax incentives upon completion of the facility. Still, Busch executives thought Fort Collins was the best place to put a brewery. It was close to I-25, it had a big university with, an emphasis on something near and dear to August Busch's heart, a world class equine center to take care of the big Clydesdales, and the city was very progressive in terms of offering amenities to its citizens. The Busch people were happy with the Lincoln Center, the trail system, and the other features that made Fort Collins such a good place to live.

In 1982, Busch secretly bought 1133 acres of land north of town. They wanted the transaction kept under wraps because they were still negotiating with Pueblo and Greeley. They bought the land through intermediaries at the Everitt Companies and spread the rumor that the land was going to be used by General Dynamics.

Fort Collins drove a hard bargain. Not only did Busch have to buy the land for its brewery, but also the city insisted that they purchase the water it would need to make their beer. Busch ended up buying 4,500-acre feet of water, which it had to deliver to the City of Fort Collins. It was many millions of dollars.

Busch got some concessions from the city. It required that the brewery be included in the city limits because they wanted the city's much cheaper rates for power. The city, did however, agree to invest the tax money it collected for ten years from Busch into the nearby infrastructure, building roads, water and sewer lines.

The State of Colorado chipped in and agreed to build a new freeway interchange in front of the brewery. That was worth $10 million.

By the end of 1983, the deal was complete. The Fort Collins city council was ready to approve the PUD for the project. Then there was a glitch. Busch planned to power the new plant with natural gas, however, there was a backup system in the event that gas supplies were interrupted. This backup system was coal-fired. That meant there could be the possibility of pollution. A study was conducted by an independent company, which said that coal pollution annually would amount to over 1300 tons. This was dramatically different from the federal EPA estimates that put the pollution at about 500 tons.

Budweiser officials met privately with every member of the city

*NOT SO EASY. The building of the Budweiser brewery was an extended and much discussed subject. The public was asked to vote on it. (Courtesy Style Magazine.)*

council. They made it clear that they would only accept a compromise pollution rate of 750 tons per year. They pointed out that this was only a backup system and would likely never be used. They told each member of the council that it they didn't get the compromise they proposed, they would move the brewery to another site.

The city council took up the matter and debated the issue for some time. Three members of the council were opposed to any compromise. They had serious doubts as to the value of such a big new company in town in the first place since it was tied to the entire growth issue. This was their way of using an environmental consideration to bottle up the project. When the vote was taken, the compromise to Busch was passed 4 to 3.

The city council majority had another problem. Serious questions had been raised in town about the brewery. There were a number of arguments. Among them was one about alcohol being produced in Fort Collins, another one was about the modest tax incentives, and another had to do with allowing such a big new employer in town to spur more growth and put additional pressure on the infrastructure.

Mayor John Knezovich was of the opinion that the city council should just pass the resolution approving the construction of the brewery, but city councilman John Clarke was certain that wasn't the right approach. Clarke argued that there was enough opposition to the plant that if the council just made the approval out of hand, that they would likely be faced with lawsuits and referendums demanding public input to the process. He favored having the council approve and endorse the project, but then immediately submit it to the voters for their approval. In this way, Clarke believed that the council could show they were sensitive to the desires of the public. Reluctantly the mayor agreed.

Budweiser was shocked to hear that their new brewery was going to be put to a vote of the people. Nothing like that had ever happened in the history of Anheuser-Busch. However, they said that if that's what it took, they would go along with the process.

The vote was scheduled for the next city election in April 1984. Both sides conducted a vigorous campaign. The opponents to the brewery used the same arguments already mentioned. Those in favor of the brewery dismissed the issue of alcohol as being a pretty big stretch of the imagination. They displayed the true nature of the deal and demonstrated what a good arrangement the city had actually achieved. Lastly, they pointed out that the economy of Fort Collins had been severely compromised by the high interest rates and the depression of the construction industry. They said that Budweiser was exactly what the city needed to give a needed economic shot in the arm. When the vote was taken, Budweiser was in.

Construction on the brewery began in the fall of 1984. 800 construc-

*A MAJOR EMPLOYER. Budweiser employees 600 workers. It also pays millions of dollars in taxes that help the city to build new services for its citizens. (Courtesy Style Magazine)*

tion jobs were created. The Fort Collins brewery was the twelfth in the Anheuser-Busch family of breweries. It wouldn't be one of the biggest, but would still have a capacity to produce 5 million barrels of beer annually. The brewery complex would occupy 122 acres of the 1133. 18 acres would be under roof in eleven buildings. The tallest structure would rise to 185 feet. Construction costs were over $300 million.

12,000 people applied for the 600 available jobs. Many of the new workers were hired from Fort Collins. The brewery was finally completed and opened in mid 1988.

# The Galloping Goose

Beginning in 1906, Fort Collins had a trolley system. In the years before the city began expanding, the trolley was a mode of transportation for most of the population. It was clean, economical, convenient, and fun. In 1918, the city took over operation of the system and replaced the old cars with the lighter, more economical Birney Safety Cars.

Three times in the next 30 years, Fort Collins residents were asked to vote on whether or not to keep the trolley running. Finally, in 1951, the city council decided, without a vote of the people, to discontinue the system. For the next 30 years, the people of Fort Collins went about their business mostly in their cars, although they never forgot how the neat little trolleys added such charm to the streets of Fort Collins. They regretted that the last of the

THE GALLOPING GOOSE. *Last of the Fort Collins trolleys; was rescued from destruction by active civic groups. It was moved from Library Park to be renovated. (Courtesy of Wayne Sundberg)*

trolleys, Old No. 21, sat forlornly in Library Park, rotting away behind a wire fence.

In 1976, The Fort Collins Junior Women's Club undertook the restoration of the last trolley, which had always gone by the nickname of "The Galloping Goose." Other more ambitious members of the community hoped that they could actually get the trolley back into service. The Fort Collins Municipal Railway Society was organized for that purpose in March 1981.

Since most of the track and the right of way were still in place along Mountain Avenue, to City Park, it was decided that this would be the perfect route for the little trolley to run.

There was almost immediate opposition to the proposal. Some of the residents along Mountain Avenue were convinced that the trolley was going to ruin their lives and devastate their property values.

*"WE DON'T WANT IT," cried some of the residents along the proposed trolley route on Mountain Avenue. They feared for their property values, and the noise of the trolley. (Courtesy of Wayne Sundberg)*

They complained that the trolley was noisy and would destroy their greenbelt. The Trolley Society patiently explained that the trolley was only going to operate a few times a day, only on weekends during the summer. They also pointed out that the trees and shrubs, which had been planted in the years since the trolley was taken out of service, could be moved and preserved. It made no difference to the minority of people opposed to the entire idea. They were led by Chuck Wanner, who lived on Mountain,

*DRIVING THE GOLDEN SPIKE. Mayor Kelly Ohlson made a fun event out of the opening of the trolley. He later said he was wrong for opposing the project. (Courtesy of Wayne Sundberg)*

and who campaigned vehemently to block the project.

By the time the proposal reached the city council, the rhetoric had become almost ridiculous. It was as if the issue of the trolley was more important than any of the other pressing matters of business for the City of Fort Collins. When the key vote was taken in 1983, councilpersons Kelly Ohlson, Gerry Horak, and Barbara Rutstein voted against the trolley. The majority overruled them. The vote was 4 to 3.

A car barn to house the trolley was built and dedicated on April 1, 1983. On December 29, 1984, after restoring the track, refitting the trolley and moving 64 trees and shrubs, the Galloping Goose made its maiden voyage down Mountain Avenue. It was not the complete system. Tracks were still several blocks short of the final terminus of the trolley in front of St. Joseph's church at Howes Street. But by the summer of 1986, the system was complete and Mayor Kelly Ohlson drove the golden spike. In the summer of 1985, over 9,000 people rode the trolley, just for fun. It has been successfully operated every summer since then. There have been well over 150,000 riders on the trolley since it was completed. The cries of noise and economic ruin to property values have disappeared. In fact, most of the residents of Mountain

*FUN SUMMER FUN. The colorful, nostalgic, and charming trolley rolls its way down Mountain Avenue every summer, to the delight of children and adults alike. (Courtesy of Wayne Sundberg)*

Avenue enjoy the nostalgic little trolley rolling by on the weekends on warm summer afternoons.

# The Rawhide Energy Station

Electricity rates in northern Colorado have always been traditionally low. This is because the cities of Fort Collins, Loveland, Longmont, and

Estes Park have their own power generating station. The four cities banded together in the 1950s to supply wholesale energy to their communities at considerable savings over buying it from the western power grid individually. The association of the four communities is called the Platte River Power Authority with directors from each city.

With the growth of the entire region, Platte River began planning to meet the energy needs of the future. By 1976, plans were advanced to build a new power station. The analysis showed that a new plant should be coal-fired to take advantage of the large supply of coal nearby in Wyoming. Platte River determined that the technology existed to insure the plant would meet or exceed any environmental considera-

HOMETOWN POWER. *The Rawhide Energy Station provides power for four northern Colorado communities, including Fort Collins. (Courtesy of John Clarke)*

tions while still remaining competitively priced. The search for a new site was begun.

Platte River found exactly the site they were looking for in December 1976. It was about 20 miles north of Fort Collins and 3 miles west of I-25. It had a convenient railhead to bring coal to the location, and the proper geology to dig a cooling reservoir. The area was marked on the geological survey maps as "Rawhide." That name was an instant success. The plant was never known as anything else. It seemed to capture exactly, the nature of the business in which Platte River was engaged.

Three years of exhaustive study were needed to determine the environmental impact of the plant. There was almost no human population of any kind in the area. Coal trains could deliver coal by the shortest route possible from Wyoming with a minimal community impact. The land was desert-like rangeland with no agricultural activities of any note being conducted on the land. The Larimer County Commissioners on March 26, 1979 gave final approval for the plant.

Groundbreaking took place in September of that year. After a construction period of five years, Rawhide Energy Station was completed. On March 31, 1984, the first watt of electricity began flowing out of the plant.

Rawhide featured a 500-acre cooling lake. Water is pumped out of the plant to be cooled by the lake. A peninsula at the north end disperses the currents of water to insure that warm and cool water is being continuously mixed together. The lake contains treated sewage water that is recycled into the plant to be reused. A constant mixture of warm and cold water keeps the temperature of the lake almost constant and the surface almost never freezes. It is a wildlife Valhalla. The lake contains fish that are so big, the employees consider a five pound bass too small to keep. Over a hundred species of birds live around the lake. There are three islands in the lake that make an even better refuge.

Cottonwood trees were planted there and the area is filled with hawks, osprey, falcons, and other raptors. Migratory birds of all kinds use the lake and the islands as refuge during their flights. The Animal

*PERFECT SETTING. Not only does Rawhide provide electricity, but also its grounds are a lively wildlife refuge for a variety of birds and animals. (Courtesy of John Clarke)*

Sciences Department at Colorado State University manages a permanent herd of almost a hundred buffalo.

The power plant itself is on the north shoe of the lake. It employees about 150 people. The air quality system removes the sulfur dioxide and fly ash from the flue gas produced by the boiler as it burns the coal. 99.7% of the dust, smoke and pollutants are removed from the burned coal.

Trains arrive with 55 cars of coal every other day. The plant maintains a 60-day supply, and 11,000 tons of coal is stored on-site. The plant burns just under a million tons of coal annually.

The result is 280 megawatts of electricity everyday. This is more than enough to supply the needs of all four cities. The excess power is dumped into the western power grid where it is sold for a profit.

# Terrorism Comes Home to Fort Collins

While the rest of the world has become accustomed to having to live with acts of terrorism, they have been rare in the United States. In fact, until the bombing of the World Trade Center, the only act of foreign terrorism ever committed in the United States was in Fort Collins.

A crime against a former CSU student in 1981 attracted worldwide attention. Faisal Zagallai was a Libyan national who was living in Fort Collins and had attended CSU. He was widely known to oppose the government of Moammar Khadafy. He made no secret of the fact that he felt his government was responsible for the miseries of the country and that Khadafy was no more than a gangster who preyed upon the people.

A man named Eugene Tafoya, of Truth or Consequences, New Mexico, arrived in town during the summer of 1981. He went to the home of Zagallai and a fight ensued. During the fight, Zagallai was shot in the head twice. The first news out about this incident was that it was just a domestic shooting. This was serious enough to make a lot of news in Fort Collins, but nothing compared to the story that began to unfold during the investigation.

Investigators pieced together their alleged story like this. A renegade ex CIA agent named Edwin Wilson hired Tafoya. Wilson was himself already under indictment for supplying arms and military hardware to Libya. He was also suspected of supplying explosives to be used in terrorist activities. Wilson hired Tafoya to come to Fort Collins and shut Zagallai up since his publicity of Libya's involvement with terrorist activities was embarrassing for the Khadafy regime. Tafoya was arrested for shooting Zagallai, who recovered, but lost the sight in one eye. Tafoya was charged with first-degree attempted murder and conspiracy.

The trial began on December 5, 1981. Tafoya testified that he believed that he had been hired by the CIA itself and sent to Fort Collins to go to Zagallai's apartment and rough him up. He said he had no orders to kill and that the shooting was done in self-defense. The prosecution tried to tie Tafoya to Wilson, but there was just not enough evidence to connect the two. There was also no evidence that the CIA had any involvement in the incident and the prosecution doubted they would have been involved in the first place since they had never supported Khadafy under any circumstances.

The entire trial was loaded with cloak and dagger testimony. The Fort Collins jurors tried to sort it all out and weigh the facts based on exactly what they heard in credible testimony. When they returned with their verdict, Tafoya was convicted of third-degree assault and conspiracy to commit the same. They said that they believed Tafoya when he said he had not gone to Zagallai's apartment to kill him. Tafoya was sentenced to 2 and half years in jail. He posted an appeal bond of $10,000 after spending only five hours in jail following the conviction. He then slipped out of town and the case died a quiet death.

Fort Collins just couldn't believe that the big, bad world had actually come to their community. But it had. Nothing like that had ever happened before.

# Thomas Sutherland is Kidnapped

A much more real and heart wrenching drama began playing out in 1985. On June 9th, Dr. Thomas Sutherland, a CSU professor was kidnapped and abducted by the Islamic Jihad, known as the Hezbollah.

Sutherland was born and raised on a diary farm in Falkirk, Scotland. After immigrating to the United States he obtained his Ph.D. from Iowa State and chose to become an American citizen. He came to CSU in 1958, where he taught agriculture. He was a very popular and colorful professor. Each year on the occasion of poet Robert Burns birthday, Sutherland would show up for class wearing a full set of kilts and spend the hour reading Burn's poetry in his native Scottish brogue. His teaching style was lively and interesting. His students admired and respected him.

QUIETER TIMES. Dr. Tom Sutherland in the years before his capture, was an active teacher and researcher at CSU. This was his mouse project. (Courtesy of Tom Sutherland)

In 1964, he was selected as CSU's favorite professor.

Dr. Sutherland was dedicated to serving the poverty stricken people of the world. He spent two years as the training director for the International Livestock Center in Ethiopia.

Sutherland met his wife, Jean, while they were both students at Iowa State. Together they had three daughters, Ann, Kit, and Joan. Jean Sutherland was also a teacher of English studies.

In 1983, Sutherland took a three-year leave of absence from CSU to accept the position of Dean of Agriculture at the American University of Beirut in Lebanon. His wife Jean went along to teach English.

Through 1983, 1984, and early 1985, the situation in Lebanon deteriorated almost on a daily basis as the country fell to the illogical machinations of tribal warfare. The war involved Maronites, Orthodox Christians, Sunni and Shiite Muslims, the Druze, and swiftly shifting sands of the politics of the region involving Syria, Iran, Iraq and Isreal.

Sutherland's captors were the angry and desperate Shiites of Lebanon, the most radical of all the players in the region. "Hostage-taking was an easy way to make a statement," said one Washington based Middle East scholar and a Lebanese Shiite. "They want to convey to the world that they are angry with Isreal, the United States, and the Lebanese State."

This long-suffering group was divided into two factions: the moderate Amal and the more radical Hezbollah. This was the group that would hold Thomas Sutherland captive for nearly 6 and a half years.

In their book, "*At Your Own Risk,*" Tom and Jean Sutherland told the story of their ordeal in brilliant, poignant detail. The Sutherland's had been home in Colorado for a short vacation and the graduation of their daughter after which he returned to Lebanon. After landing at Beirut Airport, he was being

A CITY AT SIEGE. *Beirut, Lebanon blew apart into fighting among many factions. The Shiite Moslem group, Hezbollah, held Sutherland hostage. (Courtesy Tom Sutherland)*

driven back to the university. Here is how Tom Sutherland described the kidnapping.

*West we went, into the sunset, Sharif, and I eagerly exchanging respective news. Suddenly I became conscious of a little brown Simca drawn alongside of us, uncomfortably close, windows rolled down and four young men staring ominously at us. "Who are you?" barked a little fellow in the right rear seat, wearing a baseball cap turned backward like a catcher. Strange. Never seen these characters in my life before. Why should they want to know who I am? CRASH. Sideswiped, by God! Then CRASH. Sideswiped again! I should have smelled a rat when they first approached and ordered Sharif, "Go -go. Get out of here!" His powerful Caprice could easily have outrun that clunker little Simca. Too late. They darted in front of us, cut us off, Sharif jammed on the brakes and we all came to a dead stop, including Dr. Ayash ahead and Naih Zaidan behind. The four young men poured out of the Simca. Another four appeared from a second car behind it. Eight men in their late teens/early twenties, each carrying a submachine gun he promptly started to use. What a bloody racket! Bullets flying everywhere spewing into the tar of the road and into our car - ricocheting in all directions as the men danced excitedly around our car. "Good Lord, what's going on, Sharif?" I muttered in disbelief. Eyes dilated, obviously nervous and hyped up - so were we by this time. "Get out of the car," ordered young Baseball Cap, appearing at my side and pulling open the door of the Caprice. I didn't argue with him. He still had a red-hot machine gun in his hands, and the words of advice from the American embassy suddenly flooded into my mind, "Don't be a hero. Don't resist. Do what they*

WE NEVER FORGOT. *Fort Collins changed the yellow ribbons on their trees and homes many times, but they never forgot that one of their own was being held hostage. (Courtesy Tom Sutherland)*

*say and maybe you'll live."*

The nightmare had begun.

In Fort Collins the word passed quickly. One of our own had been taken hostage. The next day yellow ribbons started to appear on trees all over town. They were replaced many times. The people of Fort Collins hungered for every scrap of news, but there was always precious little. About all the people knew for sure was that Thomas Sutherland was alive, but was still being held by the Hezbollah.

# A Troubled Economic Picture

The year 1980 was the highest inflation year for America in modern history. The rate topped 13.5% that year. Other economic factors were to plague Fort Collins through much of the decade and had a chilling effect on the construction and home buying industry. Progress was not stopped, but it was certainly restricted.

From 1981 until 1983, there was a depression in land values in Fort Collins. Developer Bill Neal remembers, "Lots in Brown Farm were selling for $18-20 thousand in the late 70s, by 1982 the same lots were selling for $9-10 thousand."

This was just a taste of the hard times that would follow. In 1983, lots in the upscale Landings subdivision were completely depressed. On Whalers Way, you could buy a lot for $4,500.

The picture was not very encouraging. Prime interest rates were 20 to 21%, and home mortgages were 18%. The high flying gas and oil industry that had led the way in Colorado in the 1970s collapsed. Oil prices were tumbling. Oil had been selling for $30-40 a barrel in the late 70s, but by 1983 was down to $16-18 a barrel. Finally, the agricultural industry was not doing well. Farm prices were severely depressed and foreclosures were on the rise.

In the mid 1980s three major events had a profound effect on commercial properties. They certainly were factors in the difficulties Gene Mitchell experienced in Old Town.

First, was the passage of the Gallagher Act in Colorado in 1985. This fundamental change in the way property taxes were assessed shifted the burden of taxes from residential to commercial property. The Gallagher Amendment said that 55% of the property taxes would come from commercial property and 45% would be derived from residential taxes. However, there was a cap on the increase that could be assessed on residential properties, but no such limitation on commercial property. The result was a growing gap between the amount of state revenue that was received from commercial compared to residential property. By the end of the 20th century, Colorado had one of the lowest residential property rates in the country while having nearly the highest commercial rates.

Next, was a big change in the Federal Tax Code. This change removed the deduction on personal and corporate income taxes for commercial and investment real estate. Investors who had been holding rental property and taking a loss on the monthly rents, but recovering it in tax deductions could no longer do this. The result was that proper-

BIG BOX. *The major retail discount stores had discovered Fort Collins too. Their lower prices made staying in business for the independent retailers a tough job. (Courtesy Style Magazine)*

ties had to have a positive cash flow in order to be profitable. Hundreds of rental and commercial properties in Fort Collins were thrown onto the real estate sales market and sold, often for a loss.

Finally, was the arrival of the Big Box. These were the giant corporate chains that wanted to capitalize on the population growth of Fort Collins. This included the K-Marts, Wal-Marts, chain grocery stores, and other major discount retailers who could buy for less, and sell for less. The small, independently owned businesses could not compete and many of them were forced out of business.

An example of this was seen in the two developments at Shields and Drake with the Raintree and Cimarron commercial centers. When they were built, building costs were about $25 a foot, not including the land. This escalated to a high of about $75 a foot before the changes in the laws and the arrival of the Big Boxes. By 1988, the total appraised value of both developments had tumbled to $18 a foot.

For a while, the developers got around these limitations by forming Special Improvement Districts where their projects were financed through bonds, often guaranteed by the City of Fort Collins. When the

NEW CITY GOLF COURSE. *The city hadn't planned it that way, but they still ended up being the owner of the Southridge Golf Course. (Courtesy Style Magazine)*

developers fell behind on their payments, the bond companies fore-closed on the land and demanded payment. This was the case in at least two instances in Fort Collins. One of them was in Southeast Fort Collins where the city ended up owning the Southridge Golf Course. The other project was the big development of Provincetown. The developers had used bond money to put in the streets and roads, but when they defaulted on the bond, the city was forced to take over the project because they had guaranteed the bonds to get the streets, utilities, curbs, and gutters built.

In the end, CSU saved Fort Collins and helped to support the economy. The University was mostly insulated from the economics of the times. Enrollment continued to rise and jobs continued to expand. The ability of CSU to inject needed cash into retail sales was the single factor that kept Fort Collins from getting into real trouble.

## There's No Business like Snow Business

In 1983, there was a big snowstorm in Fort Collins. There was nothing particularly remarkable about that. It snows every year along the Front Range. However, this storm created a storm all by itself. City councilman Kelly Ohlson was in Portland attending a Conference of Cities forum. His brother called him from Fort Collins and complained vehemently that the snow was too deep to drive his car down his street so he could get to work. Ohlson asked whether the city snowplows had plowed the street. The answer was "no." Ohlson wanted to know if his brother had called the city to find out when the street was going to be plowed. The answer was that the city had no plans to plow the street at all. Ohlson called the city manager and asked about getting the streets plowed. He was told that plowing the streets was the job of the city transportation department and that the city would handle all

SNOWED IN. *When a colossal snowstorm gripped Fort Collins in 1985, the public screamed for help and the eager city council went to their aid. (Fort Collins Public Library)*

ordinary work of that type and that a city councilman should not concern himself with routine city business, leaving that to the city manager to manage.

Ohlson thought about this for a minute and then said, "City councilpersons respond to the concerns of the public. The public is concerned that it can't go about their normal lives, go to work, take the kids to school, go shopping and so forth, because they can't get out of their driveways, because the city hasn't plowed the streets. I think this is my business."

The city manager thought about that for a minute and then he said, "If the city council is going to start messing around with the way that the staff runs the city on every petty point, we're never going to get anything done."

And the fight was on.

For just about as long as anyone could remember, the city manager and his staff were the principal directors of operations for the city of Fort Collins. If you wanted to do something; build a house, open a business, have a parade, run an event, or any of a hundred other day by day activities, the city staff was the last word. The role of the city council was to direct the overall policy of the city, and implement new programs and projects. They would turn over the entire matter to the staff who would take care of everything.

Fort Collins was evolving. The people were no longer willing to stand by and let everything happen around them without having a say in the process. The people became much more proactive in their approach to government and didn't hesitate to express their opinions to their elected representatives.

Those who were being elected to the city council were of a like mind. This was particularly true beginning with the city election in 1983. That council was a notable bunch of young lions. Their average age could not have been more than 35 years. Clarke, Ohlson, Horak, Rutstein, Stoner, Knezovich, and Miller were filled with the zeal to have a profound effect on city government and had the youthful energy to do it.

Very early in the process this energetic council found out that the city manager, city staff, and the general apparatus of government was not ready or willing to accept this approach. They frankly resented all this meddling in their day to day business.

YOUNG LION. Kelly Ohlson. Mayor of Fort Collins in 1986-87. One of the new breed of city council members who changed the way Fort Collins was governed. (Courtesy of Kelly Ohlson)

This might have seemed revolutionary to the Fort Collins staff, but it was the sign of the times. All over America, city councils were moving in and taking over. In fact, at the national meeting of city managers, there was a special session devoted to dealing with these proactive councils that were very invading their territory.

Of course, it was an uneven battle. The city managers had no choice but to adjust to this new trend. After all, most of them were hired by their city council and served at their pleasure. If they didn't start cooperating and accommodating, they would find themselves out of job. Still, it was very difficult for many of them and there was a general shuffling of city managers in quite a few towns all over the country during the 1980s.

This takes us back to the snowplow incident.

In 1983, Fort Collins owned two snowplows. The general practice was to plow the main arterials and let the sun do the snow removal for the rest of the community. That was no longer going to be adequate. The people wanted an improvement in service. The city council demanded it. They pointed out to the city manager that they weren't

*SEAT OF GOVERNMENT. The Fort Collins City Hall. It is the third city hall used by government since the opening of the modern era in 1950. (Courtesy Style Magazine)*

telling the city what kinds of snowplows to buy, how many people should be put on the job, or what the schedule should be to do the work. This was the job of the city staff, and the council couldn't care less how it was done, just that it was done. The city manager reflected this increase in service by increasing the next budget. The council approved the new costs and the result was that Mrs. Citizen could get out of her neighborhood, and get the kids to school on time.

But the change in attitude and the nature of the relationship between the city staff and the council was altered forever. A much more subtle and profound change came as a result of this reshuffling of priorities. In a very short period, the attention of the people was focused on the city council itself. A whole range of social, economic, procedural, and general matters of policy were concentrated in the hands of the seven men and women who were elected to the city council. It was a fundamental change that would ring down through the years and is still the case in Fort Collins today. It's true that Fort Collins city councils have always been the voice of the people. However, the council started moving beyond that and into even more influence where they were met with reactions that ranged from enthusiastic approval to widespread disgust.

# This Space Is Open

After 1950, the population of Fort Collins was all not concentrated within the city limits of Fort Collins. A large number of people wanted something unique for a home site. It began with the building of some luxury homes overlooking Horsetooth Reservoir. Huge lots, in a natural setting, with the reservoir and the mountains as a backdrop. For many people this was heaven. But when the homes began to creep over the top of the ridge and appear on the skyline there began to be serious doubts about whether or not people ought to be able to build their homes in such a way that it cluttered up the view for everyone else. Of course, this brought the private property issue to the forefront. The Western mentality held that private property was a non-negotiable right and that nobody could tell anyone how they conducted their business on their own land. Still, the thought of having the entire foothills west of Fort Collins filled with homes was more than most people could bear.

This simple imperative gave rise to the growing concept of open space. For some time, other Colorado towns and counties had been setting aside rather large tracts of land on which no development was permitted. Jefferson County led the pack in that respect and have, to date, invested almost a billion dollars in open space. Boulder County was also a leader in this regard, but went one step further with the concept and used it as a means of growth control. The people of Fort Collins though very suspicious of that motive, could see some benefit, however.

Public parks were fine, and Fort Collins wanted a lot of those, but they were expensive to build and to maintain. Taking the logic a little further, there were areas, relatively close to Fort Collins where natural wonders and unique ecostructures existed. They weren't really park material, but should be preserved. A simple and very visible example of this was Horsetooth Mountain. Nobody could stand the idea of a house on top of that rock. It was obscene! So, a group of dedicated preservationists took it upon themselves to lobby for the establish-

*IT'S BEAUTIFUL AND ITS OURS. The emerging open spaces of Fort Collins and northern Colorado are being used and appreciated for their unique and colorful character. (Courtesy Style Magazine)*

ment of an Open Space program.

This movement developed the concept of city or county purchased open space to preserve valuable lands in behalf of its aesthetics, and separation. Fort Collins and Loveland were growing closer and closer to each other, year by year. The truth is that Fort Collins didn't want to be a part of Loveland and Loveland didn't want to be a part of Fort Collins. The immediate example of how awful this idea was took only a glance at the overlapping cities of Southern California. The Open Space committee launched a campaign to add a quarter cent of sales tax to the city sales tax and use the money to buy a corridor of land between Fort Collins and Loveland. It would be open space forever, and the two cities would preserve their integrity as separate entities.

In 1984, a vigorous campaign to pass the Open Space proposal was conducted. It was loudly and heavily attacked by a large number of people. The principal point man for the movement was Kelly Ohlson, Fort Collins City councilman. He was chided by the *Coloradoan Newspaper* as being very naive to believe that people would be willing to pay money in the form of a sales tax to preserve open space.

The result of the election was that the Open Space proposal was defeated handily.  Its time had still not come for Fort Collins and the battle would have to wait for a more appropriate time.

# The City Goes Political

After the breakneck pace of the early 1980s, which was only a continuation of the momentum that had been a part of the fabric of life in Fort Collins for 20 years, some issues had to be faced.  The city continued to grow just as fast as it had for all those years, but some of the people were becoming restless over all the changes and believed that a reorganization of basic systems was in order.  There were also social issues that were growing in importance, and the public wanted to have debates about them.  So, a dizzying series of public votes were set in motion on every subject imaginable.

It began at the end of 1979 when the public was faced with the citizen initiated ordinance that would have limited growth in Fort Collins in a fashion that was similar to Boulder.  The people said no to that very firmly.  This was not the general direction in which they intended to go.  They also did not pass an ordinance that would have decriminalized the use of marijuana.

In 1980, a citizen initiated ordinance was brought forward in a special election asking for a 1 cent sales extension on the DT squared sales tax that would provide for an indoor swimming pool, ice rink, bike paths and trails.  This was hotly contested, but defeated, as was the council initiated ordinance that would prohibit the sales tax extension but required that a pool, ice rink and bike paths be built.  Another citizen-initiated ordinance decriminalizing marijuana was defeated.

A special election in March 1981 allowed for the creation of the Downtown Development Authority, and in the regular election the following month, the voters approved a council initiated ordinance to issue general obligation bonds.  They also elected four new members to the city council; Gary Cassell, Bill Elliot, Gerry Horak, and John Knezovich.

In 1983, the voters elected Kelly Ohlson, John Clarke, and Barbara Rutstein to at-large seats on the council, and defeated a citizen-initiated ordinance to add three-quarters of a cent sales tax.  An extremely important charter amendment proposal was included in the list of charter changes.  This one would allow, for the first time, for citizen initiated resolutions to be voted on by the public.  Up until this time, the only way to express an opinion or get anything changed was through an ordinance.  The new resolution provision did not have the force of law, but everyone

BATTLEGROUND. *The EPIC Center. Often fought over by citizens to build or expand, and then fought over by the swarms of users who keep the center operating nearly around the clock, seven days a week. (Courtesy Style Magazine)*

recognized that it would be political suicide to ignore a vote of the people on a given subject.

The following year a special election was held on May 1, to consider the annexation and approval of the Anheuser-Busch Brewery. That was approved. The city was also successful in getting two quarter cent sales tax increases. One was for the construction of the EPIC center with the indoor pool and the ice rink. The other quarter cent was for capital improvements that including the building or expansion of roads. Although the EPIC center was hotly contested and was a narrow winner, when the center was finally completed it was an immediate success and started being used around the clock, seven days a week to meet the needs of skaters especially. The Fort Collins Hockey Club and Ice-Skating Club had literally thousands of participants. The voters said no by 300 votes to a citizen-initiated resolution showing opposition to nuclear weapons testing. This was the first time the new resolution ordinance to the city charter was used.

Again, in 1984, at the general election in November, nearly all the registered voters in Fort Collins voted on the new ordinance regulating smoking in public places. This ordinance made more smoke, so to speak, than just about everything else on the ballot. It had widely based support from the city council. Councilpersons Ohlson and Horak supported it, as did councilpersons Clarke and Knezovich. It was hardly possible to find two pairs of political officials who had more disagreement in policy than these four men. Yet, on the subject of limiting smoking in public places, they were true allies. The ordinance passed easily.

1985 saw three elections, one regular, and two specials. The regular election was in March and elected four city council persons. One special election in June saw the defeat of the Oak Street residential project from tax increment funding through the DDA. The second special election came with the general election in November and the voters defeated the first effort to fund open space. It was an issue that would be a recurring theme far into the next decade.

*The Larimer County Justice Center opened in late 2000*
*by Lydia Dody*

# Summoning The Future
# The 1990s

The 1990s in Fort Collins were a clash of lifestyles. On the one hand, the city continued to experience a great deal of growth and the community's prosperity has never been better. The city was the envy of the country in many ways. The periodical book, *Retirement Places Rated*, announced that Fort Collins is the number one community in the country in which to retire. On the other hand, active groups, who sought ways to effect the subjects that were closely tied to Quality of Life, brought social issues to the forefront. The underlying substance of public debate was growth, traffic, open space, and the environment.

## The 1990s At A Glance

1990    • Fort Collins population is 87,758.
         • Voters agree to elect council members by district and elect mayor by popular vote.

1991    • Thomas Sutherland is released from captivity.

1992    • First Open Space tax is approved by the voters.

1995    • Fort Collins Senior Center is built.

1997    • The Spring Creek Flood devastates the city and CSU.
         • Building Community Choices is the largest capital improvement-project in Fort Collins history.

1999    • Voters reject $90 million public transportation proposal.
         • Voters approve construction of Wal-Mart Supercenter.
         • Voters reject truck bypass on Vine Drive.

# He's Free!

In many ways, the Hezbollah held Fort Collins hostage for over six years. The scant news that dribbled out of Lebanon was gobbled up by the community and retold in hundreds of homes, offices, and restaurants. There were ups and downs as more hostages were taken and some were eventually released. But never Tom. Fort Collins watched with interest as Reverend Benjamin Weir, David Jacobsen, Robert Polhill, Frank Reed, and Edward Tracy, all were released. By the beginning of 1991, five hostages remained. They were: Terry Waite, taken January 20, 1987, Alann Steen taken January 24, 1987, Joseph Cicippio, taken September 12, 1986, the man who had been held the longest, Associated Press reporter Terry Anderson, taken March 16, 1985, and Tom Sutherland, taken two months later on June 9, 1985.

Tom's wife Jean remained in Beirut during nearly all of the time of his captivity. She continued to live and work at the American University of Beirut, teaching English and continuing the work she and her husband had started to do when they arrived in 1983. She was never bitter. "It doesn't do you any good," she would often tell the press. The family back in the United States felt the same. The Sutherland's youngest daughter, Kit, continued to live and work in Fort Collins where she was a physiology research assistant at CSU. Her lively, upbeat manner made her a darling with the media.

For Sutherland himself, life was an endless ordeal. In this book, *At Your Own Risk*, he writes:

*"The guard escorted me down a short flight of stairs, turned to the right, marched a few yards, and opened a door. I was pushed unceremoniously into a small cage or crowded stall in which a mattress had already been placed. The mattress took up the entire space, so it was roughly six feet by two and a half feet. The guard left after locking the door, and I looked around me - this cage was roughly the size of a horsebox, and barely high enough for me to stand. The roof was made of a very heavy mesh, the kind used during the war to make temporary airport runways, and the sidewalls were made of steel. Several stalls in a row. I could make out perhaps two others to the left of me, but many more off to the right. Soon the guard was back, with a piece of really rusty chain, the weight of a good strong dog chain, and proceeded to padlock my ankle to one of the bars in the bottom of the gate to my stall. Amazing. Why on earth would it be necessary to chain me to the gate in a steel stall with barely enough room for me to lie down in? My God, I thought. What kind of powers of reason do these fellows have anyway?"*

The years went by. The yellow ribbons of the trees and buildings of Fort Collins were changed many times. Tom Sutherland was a hurt that

TENDER MOMENT. *Children, who had been barely born when Tom Sutherland was captured, celebrate his return. (Courtesy of Tom Sutherland)*

just wouldn't go away.

Then one day, in November 1991, Sutherland wrote:

*"I had just begun to listen to the three o'clock news on the BBC Terry was working on his poems quietly in his head and TW (Terry Anderson) was relaxing on his mattress to my left. Suddenly the words that I had been waiting six and a half years to hear. 'We have some good news for you today?' 'Today, Mr. Waite and Mr. Sutherland go home' 'Yaba-daba-do,' I cheered. 'When today?' 'At six o'clock,' came back the reply. I could hardly believe my ears.*

*Later I was led down a long hall and out into the fresh air. Terry Waite and I were bundled into the trunk of a car,*

*first me, then Terry on top of me, all 280 pounds of him. I didn't care. I was on my way to freedom.*

*We were let out on a side road. Now what happens? Suddenly, out of the shadows a figure. 'Welcome to freedom,' came the friendly voice in well-nigh-perfect English. ' My name is General Baaloul of Syrian Intelligence. I have come to take you to freedom!'"*

With that, Thomas Sutherland was on his way home. He was first transported to Damascus. He talked to his wife Jean, on the phone in Syria and learned that she had left Beirut only the day before to go back to Iowa for the funeral of her father. Then it was on to Wiesbaden, Germany for a medical check and debriefing.

THE TRIUMPH OF FREEDOM. *Tom Sutherland celebrates his release with enthusiasm. His daughter Kit is with him as they arrive home. (Courtesy of Tom Sutherland)*

The entire family met him there and had a joyous reunion.

After stops in Iowa to attend the funeral of Jean's father and another in Oakland to see daughter Joan, who was nine months pregnant, the Sutherland's were on their way home to Fort Collins. It was December 1, 1991.

*"The view of the Rocky Mountains was spectacular - for us this time a real John Denver 'Rocky Mountain High.' Swooping down to land at the Fort Collins/Loveland Airport, we could see a huge crowd of people gathered all around, who gave us a clamorous welcome, including sky divers with American flags, flyovers by Air Force jets, hundreds of yellow signs carried by everyone saying 'Welcome Home, Tom' An enormous stretch limousine, two blocks long, this too with a huge sign of welcome attached all along the side of the vehicle, awaited us. Here I met my old friend Frank Vattano - and Bill West, a new one, whom I had never met but who, I learned, had worked tirelessly for years for me, and had worked to help arrange everything that was to come for the next several hours."*

Thousands of people lined the road for 12 miles all the way to Fort Collins, down College Avenue and into the campus at CSU. The oval was filled to overflowing with people carrying signs and banners and cheering.

Governor Roy Romer, Senator Hank Brown, Congressman Wayne Allard, and Fort Collins Mayor Susan Kirkpatrick received Sutherland

*MOBY MADNESS. A standing room only crowd awaited Sutherland at Moby Gym. The ovation upon his introduction went on for ten minutes. (Courtesy of Tom Sutherland)*

on the steps of the administration building.  Sutherland made a small speech of thanks and then was whisked off to Moby Gym where 10,000 more people were waiting to hear him.  A thunderous ovation drowned out the sound of 80 bagpipes.  The Jean and Kit Sutherland took the microphone and said,  "And now, we all give you Tom Sutherland!"

The crowd cheered for ten minutes.  Then Sutherland took the mike and began to relate the story of his 2,354 days of captivity.

Sutherland was amazingly unharmed mentally or physically by his captivity.  He seemed to take it all in stride, and almost immediately was back at work at CSU, doing what he loved best of all...teaching.

In September 1993, Tom and Jean Sutherland returned to Beirut.  This time they went with an NBC news crew to chronicle his days in captivity and to remember.  Sutherland was just as unconcerned about his safety then as he was on the day he was captured.

Tom Sutherland is a true Fort Collins hero.

# Fort Collins Stays Involved in Public Policy

Perhaps the charter amendment with the most far-reaching implications for the future of Fort Collins was held in the general election in November 1990.  This provided that city council members would no longer be elected at large, but would be selected from districts in the city.  Only the mayor would be directly elected by a vote of the majority of the people.  The result of this form of voting made it possible for a smaller number of voters to select a city councilperson who would then vote on matters for the entire city.  Almost immediately, it caused problems among some residents who felt that too few voters were selecting city councilpersons, and the

*OPEN FOR BUSINESS.  The Open Space proposal of 1992 was passed by the voters and Fort Collins was in the land preservation business.  It proved to be a popular choice.  (Courtesy Style Magazine)*

only choice they had in choosing the policy makers for the city was the representative for their district and the mayor.

The following year, 1991, Fort Collins elected their first mayor directly. Up until this time, the mayor had been selected from members of the city council. Susan Kirkpatrick had the honor of being the first elected mayor of Fort Collins. Also in the 1991 election, voters turned down a request for a second sheet of ice at the EPIC Center.

In the general election of 1992, two citizen initiated ordinances appeared on the ballot. Both of them were given no chance of passing by political pundits. One was for a new horticulture center and city zoo. The other was a return of the open space and the natural areas proposal that had been badly defeated in 1988.

As predicted, the horticulture center and zoo was completely discounted by the voters. They saw no reason whatsoever to spend precious sales tax dollars on proposals that were considered to be totally superfluous to the city infrastructure.

The natural areas proposal had the support of a wide number of environmental groups. They worked tirelessly to sell the idea of buying land to preserve for all times and to provide a corridor between Fort Collins and Loveland. Former mayor Kelly Ohlson was the prime mover for open space. Against all odds, the voters approved the natural areas proposal and a full quarter-cent was added to the sales tax.

In 1995, a reworked proposal for city parks and the second sheet of ice for the EPIC Center came back to the voters. Once again, the voters were in no mood to spend sales tax money on these projects. The arguments put forth by the Fort Collins Hockey and Figure Skating groups that the EPIC ice center was being used around the clock nearly every day of the year fell on deaf ears.

# The Great Timberline Debate

The last of the "Choices 95" projects called for the construction of a bridge over the Poudre River as an extension of Timberline Road. There was no question that a new crossing over the river was needed. The expansion of the city to the south and east had made for a lot of traffic across town. People were forced to drive either to I-25 or to Lemay to find a way across the river. This was inconvenient, to say the least, and it put a disproportionate amount of traffic on Lemay. The construction of the new Fort Collins High School at Timberline and Horsetooth made the need even greater. With funding in hand, the city proceeded to make plans to build the bridge.

Murmurings of discontent and then outright cries of objections broke

*ALONG TIMBERLINE. The new Fort Collins High School at the corner of Timberline and Horsetooth is one of the reasons why the Timberline extension was necessary. (Courtesy Style Magazine)*

out in certain quarters of Fort Collins. Soon, the Timberline extension was all tied up in the growth debate. Those who were opposed to the bridge cited environmental objections. They pointed out that this portion of the river was part of the city's natural areas. There were a number of small ponds near where the bridge would be built. Although these were not naturally occurring ponds, they were created when companies mined the area for its gravel and sand; they nevertheless developed into a useful habitat for wildlife. The entire area had been largely undisturbed for a number of years, and the environmentalists were worried that the building of the bridge would create a major disruption.

Of course, the fact that the new road would create a major umbilical to the north and facilitate new growth in those areas was part of the

*PRETTY NATURAL. The River Bend ponds were created when the gravel was mined. They quickly became wildlife habitats and were along the route of the Timberline extension. (Courtesy Style Magazine)*

157

*A BETTER BIKE TRAIL. One of the adjustments made in building the bridge at Timberline were bike paths set back from the river to keep from disturbing wildlife. (Courtesy Style Magazine)*

unspoken agenda.

The debate went on for months. There were times when it looked like the bridge would never be built. One objection after another was raised, ranging from the size of the bridge to the location of the bike trail nearby. There were also some practical considerations. How would the bridge be protected from a flood of the river? What would be done with the Dry Creek drainage that was nearby? What kinds of development would be permitted along Timberline Road leading to the bridge?

In the end, City Manager John Fischbach brought in a young colleague of his from Vancouver, Washington, and assigned him the task of addressing all the objections. Darren Atteberry attacked the problem with single-minded determination. The money to build the bridge was already in place, approved by the voters. The need was critical, but so were the other considerations that had been brought up. Atteberry stuck his finger in the biggest hornet's nest in town and started tackling the issues one by one.

He negotiated a change to the bike path that drew it away from the river a considerable distance to produce less of an impact on wildlife. He set up boundaries around the Riverbend ponds to protect those areas. He worked with engineers to make the most durable, quiet and modern bridge possible. He even had a system installed that would apply a biodegradable liquid to the surface of the bridge to keep it from freezing and becoming slick in cold weather. Over a period of several months, Atteberry addressed each of the objections. The project went forward. Toward the end of the summer of 1996, all the hard work paid

*THE CENTERPIECE, of all the controversy was the Timberline Bridge. Compromises between the needs of the people and the needs of the environment made it a better project. (Courtesy Style Magazine)*

off. The project was now a better one than it would have been if there had been no objections. The environmental community was still opposed to the whole project on principle, but enough of their concerns had been satisfied to be willing to accept the compromises.

The city council approved the plan, and in 1997, the bridge was completed. Left unresolved was the matter of the access road to the bridge. Timberline Road was only two lanes from Prospect Street to the river and the bridge itself would not accommodate four lanes of traffic. That battle would have to wait for another time when funding and the will were available to upgrade the traffic system.

# City Plan

Since the early 1970s, Fort Collins had expanded under the Land Development Guidance System. It was a revolutionary system in that it jettisoned the whole concept of zoning and isolating various land uses into specified areas. It was the first effort to begin mixed use of residential, commercial, and industrial land uses into more compacted districts. The LDGS won national awards for its innovations and advances in land use planning.

Beginning in 1995, the City of Fort Collins initiated a new public outreach program to explore the options of overhauling the LDGS and replacing it with something better. The something better they had in mind was based on the concepts to be found in the body of work known as "modern urbanism."

The City's position was that Fort Collins had been expanding for almost 50 years and that too much of this expansion had been in subdivisions of exclusively single family, residential homes. They believed that because of this type of construction, it created sprawl. The City went on to point out that because the residential subdivision was for the single purpose of living, that all other activities such as shopping, working and engaging in recreation required the homeowner to get into their car and drive. Since Fort Collins had reached the milestone population of over 100,000 people, cars were being driven 2 million miles per day. This created traffic problems, safety issues, air pollution, and was expensive. A national study showed that the American family was spending a full 25% of their annual income on things related to the car. Through the 90s, Fort Collins had been in one, big ugly sulk. Usually sitting in a five o'clock traffic jam on College Avenue.

The City's solution to this dilemma was to encourage growth that featured multiple uses within a district. The idea was to mix the full range of human activities, residential homes, apartments, townhouses, grocery stores, offices, and recreational facilities all within a much more compacted area, and literally all within walking distance. In any case, this plan should have cut the number of vehicle miles trav-

*NOT HERE. This is an example of a Fort Collins home that could not be built under the new guidelines of the City Plan. The garage is in the front. (Courtesy of John Clarke)*

eled on a daily basis.

Opponents of the City Plan pointed out that Fort Collins had been doing this and that in the past, developers had built what would qualify as multiple use subdivisions.  A full 45% of the homes in Fort Collins were in this category.  A good example of this was at the intersection of Drake and Lemay.  On one corner, there was Parkwood Lake with its stately, high-end homes built around it.  On another corner was the First Christian Church.  On another corner was the Scotch Pines Shopping Center with hundreds of apartments and condominiums surrounding it.  And on the fourth corner was an industrial factory at the Woodward Governor plant.  Fort Collins had already taken many steps toward the future with innovative design and "managed growth."

What the opponents really objected to was the way in which construction was supposed to occur.  The City Plan called for much smaller lot sizes, with garages on the sides or backs of the homes.  It called for narrower streets and a much denser environment.  They said that home construction should be market driven and not reflect the concepts of "social engineering."

The City began working with the development community to try and reach an agreement on the differences.  They said that the City Plan was a dynamic document and would be changed to reflect the changing times and the needs of the market place.

In 1997, City Plan was approved and adopted by the city council on a split vote.  At first, very little change came in home construction.  There were still a number of projects in the pipeline that had already been approved under the old LDGS.  But as the inventory of projects and the available lots dwindled, a few developers tried to build projects under the new City Plan.  There were many problems.  The City had insisted that the new City Plan made the approval process easier, quicker, and, therefore, cheaper.  The developers said that nothing of the kind was the case and that City Plan was a mass of regulations that were a nightmare to work through and implement.

# Growth Pays Its Own Way

The most common phrase regarding development of property in the 1990s was "Growth should pay its own way."  What that meant was that all the costs associated with the construction of a subdivision, commercial building, or industrial complex needed to be paid up front.  From the very beginning, developers have paid for the improvements associated with their construction projects.  When they built subdivisions, they were required to pay for the streets, curbs, gutters, and installation of utilities.  These were just the costs of doing business, and were always reflected in the price of the homes.

In the 1990s, this changed.  Now developers were responsible for

*LOADED WITH FEES. The new homes built in the 90s were subject to a variety of new city fees designed to make growth, "Pay its own way." (Courtesy of John Clarke)*

paying, not only these standard costs, but also the costs of whatever might be needed in that subdivision in the future. If there was a possibility that the street would need to be widened, there was a street oversizing fee. If it looked like the development was going to produce additional traffic in the future, there was a fee for that. The routine costs of future improvements or future impacts were not spread out through bonds or special assessments that could be retired over a long period of time. Rather they were paid for on the spot, as the development was built.

This was the basic premise of growth paying its own way. The problem with this system was that it significantly increased the price of the homes or buildings. In many ways, this was the mechanism that was used to slow down growth.

This was not a problem that was isolated in Fort Collins, or even Colorado. It was a national trend. Making growth pay its own way has resulted in the lowest supply of housing in America, relative to the demand, in nearly 40 years. Yet, governments seemed to spend a lot of time talking about affordable housing as if this was a market driven phenomenon. New home sales prices continued to skyrocket. In Larimer County, the median price of a new home in 1999 was $176,900. A year later the new home cost was $195,000. This was an increase of 10.23%. It was more than inflation, more than the increase of out-of-pocket costs. Municipal fees drove most of the increases.

162

Not only could people not afford to buy a home at the beginning of the new century, they couldn't afford to rent one either. In Larimer County 38% of renters couldn't afford to rent a one-bedroom apartment, 47% couldn't afford a two-bedroom apartment, and 64% couldn't afford to rent a three-bedroom apartment. This was based on the percentage of renters who needed to spend more than 30% of their gross annual income on housing.

Some people, in and out of government in Fort Collins said that residents didn't want new communities and roads built adjacent to their homes. However, a national survey taken in 2000 among randomly chosen rural and urban registered voters showed differently.

- 70% of respondents who experienced new-home construction in their area approved of it.
- 80% of those polled welcomed new road construction and widening of existing roads.
- 80% approved of new retail or shopping centers opening because of residential growth.
- 64% disapproved of any legislative requirements that would force existing neighborhoods to become denser.
- 75% were opposed to policies that would make it more difficult or expensive to drive their cars.

# Building Community Choices

Sales taxes for civic improvements are not perpetual. Nearly all of them have sunset dates. During the 1980s, several such proposals were presented to the voters. Some passed and some failed. The 1989 proposal was called Choices 95 and provided for two quarter-cent sales taxes to build streets and improve city infrastructure. An additional quarter-cent was added in 1992 for purchasing open space. This was the first time that the voters had approved such a proposal.

All of those sales taxes were due to expire at the end of 1997. The general sentiment among the city council, city staff, and a wide number of citizens was that the continuing needs of Fort Collins would have to be met. This meant that the tough job of convincing the voters of the needs would have to be undertaken.

Beginning in 1995, a series of public outreach meetings and input from a large number of community groups was initiated by the administration. The purpose of this outreach was to identify the most pressing needs of Fort Collins and to prioritize them into a package that could be offered to the public in the city elections in April 1997.

The list was long indeed. Nearly a billion dollars in improvements were identified. Obviously, this was considerably more than an extension of the three quarter-cent sales taxes could provide over any reasonable period. The difficult job of prioritizing the projects went on for almost two years.

Finally, Twenty-one projects made the cut. They were divided into three separate ordinances, each with a quarter cent sales tax fund source. Each would be voted on separately by the voters. The price tag for all the programs together was $124 million. This meant that only about 10% of the original projects on the wish list were represented. It also meant that this campaign was easily the largest capital improvements program in city history.

Help Build Our

Community Choices

without additional taxes

Vote **YES** for

NATURAL AREAS, TRAILS, AND PARKS

STREETS AND TRANSPORTATION

CAPITAL IMPROVEMENTS

WATCH YOUR MAIL FOR THE CITY BALLOT THIS MARCH

*A MIGHTY EFFORT. More than 300 volunteers spread out over the city to pass out these brochures seeking support for Building Community Choices. (Courtesy of Phil Walker)*

The list included: The Fossil Creek Community Park; a new horticulture center, money for open space and natural areas; street maintenance; the Mason Street Corridor; road improvements on Prospect and Shields Streets and Taft Hill Road; a second sheet of ice for the EPIC Center; a new Northside Aztlan Community Center; library technology improvements; and land for a new library, performing arts center, and police building.

In January 1997, a citizens group was formed and the campaign was named Building Community Choices. The general chair of the committee was Phil Walker with Bill Neal serving as co-chairman. The committee went right to work and began a substantial public information program to present the packages to the people of Fort Collins. Over 300 volunteers worked to distribute literature, and give speeches to local groups.

The city election was held on April 8, 1997. The voters approved all three of the ordinances. The margin of victory was 71% in favor of

Building Community Choices and it did not lose in a single precinct. At last, a comprehensive list of proposals had been assembled that had enough community support to motivate the voters to dedicate sales tax money to them. Building Community Choices was carefully crafted to match popular programs with projects that had been turned down in the past. The people of Fort Collins accepted the open compromises that the program offered.

# The Spring Creek Flood

On Monday night, July 28, 1997, the worst natural disaster in Fort Collins history killed five people, injured forty more, left hundreds homeless, damaged or destroyed a thousand buildings, and caused hundreds of millions of dollars in damage. It was the Spring Creek Flood.

There is an annual weather window in northern Colorado that runs from the last week of July through the first week of August. During that time, the conditions are right for a catastrophic weather event within a seventy-mile-wide strip east of the mountains, somewhere between Cheyenne, Wyoming and Denver, Colorado. John Weaver, a NOAA research meteorologist at Colorado State University and Colorado Assistant State Climatologist Nolan Doeskin had published an article on just that subject in 1990. They discovered that 28 out of the previous 30 years there had been a major weather event during this two-week period. A notable example of this was the Big Thompson Flood on July 31, 1976. Another was a huge hailstorm in Fort Collins on July 30, 1979 that

A GATHERING STORM. Great masses of warm and cold air collided over northern Colorado to produce the devastation of the Spring Creek flood. (Courtesy of John Clarke)

caused $20 million in damage and killed one person.

These weather phenomenons are produced by the summer monsoon, brisk, mid level winds that push humid air into Colorado from the Gulf of Mexico. This warm, wet air is combined with cold air that flows onto the northern plains from Canada. The two fronts collide over the Front Range and produce ferocious storms. They can be very slow moving storms that produce an upslope condition. At times the storms can stall out over the mountains or the foothills for hours or days, and dump extraordinary moisture on the usual semi-arid plains.

By Friday afternoon, July 25, 1997, it was clear to John Weaver that his little "Magic Window" was opening up again. Weaver read the weather conditions and could see that there was a lot of moisture in the air at upper levels, caused by the monsoonal flow, and an approaching cold front with an equal load of moisture at lower levels was flowing into the northern Front Range. To make matters worse, the upper level winds had almost stopped. This meant that if any storms formed; they would have all the moisture they would need to fuel them, and no wind to take them away. Weaver expected an upslope to form by the end of the weekend, midday Sunday at the latest, and last for at least 36 hours.

Denver forecasters seemed to agree. Although Saturday, July 26th was an absolutely spectacular weather day, perfect in all respects with temperatures in the 80's and nothing but thin high clouds drifting by, the forecasters could also see the a substantial rainstorm in the offing. They said so in their Saturday afternoon weather advisory.

Sunday morning was also nice, but around midday the cold front slid

WEST FORT COLLINS, was the first to feel the furry of the storm. Homes flooded all the area and emergency crews could not keep up. (Courtesy City of Fort Collins)

into Colorado and moved to the south. Intense high pressure developed several hundred miles northeast in South Dakota and that caused the clockwise flow to start moving a great deal of moisture upslope into the Poudre River Valley and Fort Collins. The weather service issued another advisory. This one was more strident and immediate. It said:

*"The combination of very moist atmosphere, light winds aloft and a weak cold front moving out of Wyoming will favor development of slow moving thunderstorms with heavy rain this afternoon and evening. A few locations could see as much as 4 inches of rain in a few hours. This could cause flash flooding of streams, dry creek beds, fields and urbanized areas. At this time heavy rains appear to be most likely on the plains, but cannot be ruled out along the foothills."*

Sunday afternoon it started to rain. It started lightly, but intensified as the evening and night wore on. By dawn on Monday, 4 inches of rain had fallen in northwestern Fort Collins and Laporte, and 9 inches of rain had fallen near the mouth of the Poudre Canyon. The National Weather Service warned that more rain was expected and that 4 more inches could fall in the next few hours. It said that this would likely cause some flash flooding.

Rain continued throughout the day on Monday, July 28th. It was a steady rain that effectively saturated the ground so that it would not hold any more moisture. What fell from then on would run off into the low-lying areas of Fort Collins. Just after 5 p.m., satellite imagery showed that the huge front, several hundred miles long, had started moving back eastward. At the same time, the upslope was becoming more intense. The low level cumulus clouds, loaded with moisture, were colliding with the high level monsoonal moisture. Worse, a new set of storm tops was heading toward Fort Collins from the south. The National Weather Service issued a Flash Flood Watch for eastern Larimer County.

All the weather factors converged in a relatively small area. Principally, the rainfall was the worst along Overland Trail between Mulberry and Drake.

The topography of Fort Collins significantly affects the way water flows through the city. On the western edge of town, the elevation is about 5,200 feet. Six miles east on the other side of town, the elevation is about 4,900 feet. That's a 300-foot drop and water will pick up a lot of speed with that kind of a gradient. Another factor is that the terrain is not flat all over the city. Water drains into several shallow drainage basins, two or three miles wide, which channels water toward the east. At the bottom of one of these basins is a usually placid tributary of the Poudre River called Spring Creek.

*DOWNHILL RUN. The rain had soaked the ground and now ran down into the Spring Creek drainage where it picked up speed and volume. (Courtesy City of Fort Collins)*

It had been raining very hard for an hour before the first emergency calls began coming into the 911 system at the Fort Collins police department. The first call came at 6:05 p.m. It was a report of a flooded basement on the west side of town. It was the first hint that serious problems were developing. Police cruisers around town began to report that intersections on the west side were starting to flood over. They also reported that it was raining extremely hard.

Within an hour, major trouble spots were developing. The Quail Hollow subdivision on the western edge of town at Overland Trail had many homeowners calling for help. They reported that their streets were flowing a foot deep in water.

The intricate system of canals, ditches, retention ponds, and sewers that crisscross Fort Collins were designed to move large amounts of water. They had a safety factor to handle a 100-year flood. This was in addition to their normal function, which was to move irrigation water to agricultural centers. These very ditches, principally the Pleasant Valley, New Mercer and Arthur Ditch, were reaching capacity and started to overflow. The retention ponds were full and they were overflowing. The sewer lines were not only full, but also beginning to be clogged with debris. The last stop gaps were failing and three to four feet of water was making its way toward the lowest level in the drainage for that part of town, Spring Creek.

The situation quickly got out of hand. By 8 p.m., the entire emergency system of Fort Collins was fully involved. Police, fire, and their entire cadre of volunteers were spread out all over the western part of town, rescuing people from flooded cars, and homes. Near the intersection of Drake and Taft Hill Road, a woman and her son had tried to drive away from the flooding waters, but their car stalled and washed away. The two tried to walk to higher ground, but by the time a fire engine arrived, they were desperately clutching a fence in ten feet of water. It took two hours for firefighters to rescue them. Similar incidents were occurring all over western Fort Collins.

Along Elizabeth Street west of the CSU campus, the intense rains had turned the street into a raging river. Police officers on the scene at 9 p.m. reported the water was nearly four feet deep and that fully loaded, very large dumpsters were "bouncing around like corks." Students were struggling to save each other using ropes, extension cords and even snowboards. Later estimates showed that the water was flowing east, into the main campus at CSU at the rate of 1,600 cubic feet per second.

Soon the intersection at Shields and Elizabeth was flooded, as were the parking lots at Moby Gym and Westfall Hall. The massive flow of water rushed east toward the Lory Student Center and the newly renovated Morgan Library. The CSU Police Department dispatch office, just east of the student center, was forced to close down and evacuate at 10:15 p.m.

The water flowed into the student center, flooding the theater. It smashed through the doors on the west side of the center and filled the basement. Then it continued toward the Oval where it filled that depression completely with the north end 8 feet under water.

At the Morgan Library, the water filled all the window wells on the west side of the building. Several of the library staff was in the basement trying to carry out what they could. Suddenly, they heard the west wall groan and begin to buckle; they ran for their lives just as the wall collapsed. The entire basement was flooded. It contained nearly a half million books. The time was 10:10 p.m.

While all of this was going on, millions and millions of gallons of water were pouring into Spring Creek. The rains were coming down in torrents and the intense core of the storm was running right down the Spring Creek Basin. Spring Creek was now a raging monster with water surging eastward at the unbelievable rate of 8,250 cubic feet per second. To better understand what this means, in order to produce that rate, Spring Creek would have to have been 40 feet wide, at least six feet deep and flowing at a rate of 25 miles per hour.

Spring Creek flowed across College Avenue near Stuart Street,

*USUALLY QUIET, but now alive and deadly, Spring Creek became a major river in only a few hours. Ultimately, the water would be running at 25 miles per hour. (Courtesy City of Fort Collins)*

through a picturesque area called Creekside Park. On the west edge of the park was the 19 foot-high railroad bed of the Burlington Northern. Between the railroad and College Avenue were two mobile home parks, the Johnson Self-storage facility, a group of residential homes, and two dozen businesses.

The people on the east side of the railroad bed were unaware that a disaster was building up on the western side of the tracks. A 50-acre lowland along Spring Creek filled first and the water began to rise as it backed up behind the raised track bed. At first, the main culvert and the seventy-eight inch overflow safety pipe that was installed for just that purpose, easily handled the flow, but soon the water began to creep up the railroad bed and eventually rose to a depth of 19 feet.

Things began to happen just after 10 p.m. A call from the fire station across College Avenue in Spring Creek Park to Fort Collins Emergency Manager Glen Levy, reported that the creek was out of its banks and had covered most of the pedestrian foot bridge. The time was exactly 10:14 p.m. Levy decided that the situation in Spring Creek Park was not as serious as other areas of town. By this time, the 911 calls were averaging one every 16 seconds. Two full shifts of dispatchers were working seven phone lines, plus all the traffic from the fire and police units. Levy had his hands full and was in the heat of the battle with 8-foot deep water in the western part of town. He couldn't give his attention to Spring Creek.

*ABOVE THE FLOOD. The Dairy Queen on South College Avenue because a refuge from residents of the mobile home parks struggling to get out of the pathway of the flood. (Courtesy of John Clarke)*

At 10:30, calls began coming into the 911 system saying that water was rising fast in Creekside Park and the mobile homes were experiencing flooding. Still, Levy and the dispatchers were so preoccupied with the disaster underway from Overland Trail to Shields, between Drake and Prospect, that they just couldn't recognize the disaster that was about to happen.

Kelly Brown, the owner of the Dairy Queen on South College and the South College Trailer Park saw the news on television at about 10 p.m. that there was flooding in town. He called the store and the manager, who had not noticed up until then, looked outside and saw water rising in the park. Brown told her to close the store and send everyone home. Then he and his son Ty jumped in their car and drove to the Dairy Queen. They arrived at about 10:15 and Kelly moved his 4 wheel drive truck up from the mobile home park to the DQ lot that was several feet higher.

By 10:30, water was beginning to rise in the mobile home park. The big pipes under the railroad bed were gushing water like a fire hose. Water was also pouring through the pedestrian tunnel. Brown sent his son to warn the residents of the trailer park. When he returned the water was starting to rise rapidly. It was now over two feet deep. Some of the residents were walking through the water toward the higher ground at the DQ.

Many of the people who lived in the two trailer parks had either gone to bed or were watching television. It had rained tremendously hard since about 8 p.m., then the rain slowed down to a normal summer storm. It seemed quiet outside, nothing out of the ordinary. Suddenly things began to happen all at once.

John Davis was watching the Rockies baseball game when he heard a "kind of deep rushing sound." He went outside to look and saw a stream of water running between his trailer and his neighbors. He thought that perhaps a water line had broken. He went back inside. The sound he had heard was water washing over gravel. The water on the west side had now risen 19 feet and was starting to flow over the top of the tracks to the east side of the embankment.

Tryg Selbo was asleep. He awakened when things began hitting the side of his trailer. As he looked outside, he saw water flowing past his front door. He took only a few minutes to gather a few possessions and his cat, but by the time he left the trailer, the water had risen waist high. Another resident who had already gotten out threw him a rope from the second floor balcony above the Breakpoint Gym and guided him to safety.

Fire prevention specialist Joe Jaramillo had gone to the fire station in Spring Creek Park to volunteer his services. No one was there. He waited a while and then drove back out to College Avenue. As he pulled up in front of the Pic-Quick Store, Jaramillo saw

*COLLEGE AVENUE becomes a river of its own as the waters of Spring Creek flood over it and closed the street to all traffic. (Courtesy of John Clarke)*

that Creekside Park was flooded. Johnson Drive was covered and the water was flowing into the Johnson Storage facility. The water looked like it was about two feet deep and rising. Jaramillo called the dispatch center and told them that the situation along Spring Creek was much more serious than they had been told until now. At 10:44, the first fire/rescue crew was dispatched to the scene.

Now the crisis was upon everyone. The water was pouring over the railroad embankment and gushing through the pedestrian tunnel, filling it to the top. The water level was now rising fast and was flowing much more rapidly. People were getting panic-stricken as they struggled through the water that was almost over their heads and was filled with debris that was knocking them off their feet. Chaos was everywhere. Mobile homes had been washed off their foundations and were floating in the rushing current toward the College Avenue bridge. Fencing, picnic tables, trees and tons of other materials were being swept along. People were mixed in with all this floating wreckage and there were heroic efforts going on everywhere to save them. The water was now as much as 12 feet deep in Creekside Park.

Things were nearly as bad on the north end of the stricken area near Prospect Street. At Johnny's Liquor Kelly Ward, A CSU senior, and employee of the store went to the basement and discovered water rushing in through the walls. In minutes, the water was two feet deep. Ward struggled to carry some computer equipment up the stairs when a loud bang came from behind him. He turned and saw the entire base-

EVERYTHING LOST. *The flood destroyed the two mobile home parks in Creekside Park. Four people died from the parks. (Courtesy of John Clarke)*

ment wall collapse and a tidal wave of water rush toward him. He scrambled up the stairs and out of the building. Then he smelled the rotten egg odor of natural gas. It was thick in the air.

Across the parking lot, people ran from the stores around Johnny's Liquor and alerted Poudre Fire Authority Battalion Chief Mel Carlson that natural gas was leaking from somewhere. It was 10:58 p.m. Fort Collins police officer Mike Goodwin was also nearby and heard the warnings of the gas leak. He quickly pulled his patrol car into the parking lot and waded out into the knee-deep water. As he walked back toward Johnny's Liquor Store, he heard the deafening sound of a train derailing. Twenty seconds later the gas ignited and blew out all the plate glass windows in the store. As he hurried to the scene he called into his radio microphone, "Johnny's Liquor has just erupted in natural gas!" It was 10:59 p.m.

When Goodwin was finally able to work his way around to the back of the liquor store, he was stunned by what he saw. Four train cars had fallen off the tracks and lay on their side. The explosion had blown the entire rear of the liquor store away. Further south, Goodwin could see the devastation in the Johnson Mobile Home Park. Deep water rushed through the park at a tremendous speed. People were clutching poles, trees, and the remains of mobile homes and screaming for help. Other voices were crying for help further south. As he stepped away from the corner of the building, he was nearly swept away by the surging current of water.

Spring Creek spilled over College Avenue and washed out the supports of the bridge. Emergency crews moved their command headquar-

THE GRIM REMAINS. What used to be two trailor parks is now just debris against the bridge on College Avenue. (Courtesy of John Clarke)

174

ters, several times to get out of the pathway of the raging flood. The streets were blocked off and emergency equipment littered the entire area. The grim business of saving as many people of possible went on furiously.

For the next several hours, nobody thought, nobody planned, everyone prayed. Firefighters, police, and volunteers struggled to bring people to safety. They plucked them off the tops of houses, out of trees and snatched them from the swirling waters. People were trapped in their mobile homes, barely holding their heads above the water. Rescuers broke windows and pulled them to safety. Small boats were launched and people were pulled dripping and nearly drowned from the angry waters.

Hours later, the dawn finally broke, and the exhausted crews could survey the scene. The rain had stopped and the waters had receded. Officials estimated that 14 inches of rain had fallen in the storm. What was left was a sight beyond belief. Dozens of mobile homes were scattered throughout the area. Many of them smashed to kindling against the College Avenue bridge. Trees had been uprooted. Furniture, clothes, appliances, cars, trucks, trailers; everything imaginable lay imbedded in the mud and silt left behind by the awful flood.

As the day progressed, Fort Collins rolled up its sleeves and went to work. Thousands of people came forth with offers to help. There was need and misery everywhere. The Red Cross operated shelters. The State of Colorado and the Federal Emergency Management Agency moved in. Fort Collins was declared a disaster area. For days, the work of cleaning up the worst of the destruction went on.

When the passage of time allowed a perspective on the Spring Creek Flood, the toll was high indeed. Five people had died in the flood. Four of them from the two mobile home parks and a fifth further down the Spring Creek drainage. Over 40 people had been seriously injured. A thousand homes and buildings had been destroyed or damaged. The losses to property were stupendous. Over a half million books at the Morgan Library had been destroyed. CSU estimated that their loses would top $135 million. Property damage in Fort Collins was over $100 million.

The Spring Creek Flood of 1997, changed everyone's life in some way, and Fort Collins added a gruesome new chapter to its history.

# Politics Gets Personal

The 1997 city election proved to be a radical departure from the character of elections in the past. In this election, city council members with clear opposition to growth and with an interest in a wider range of subjects they believed a city council should take up were elected.

The first example of the way this would be put into practice came in 1998 when the council took up the issue of the Human Rights Ordinance. The old ordinance, under which the city had been operating for two decades, needed to be modernized and updated. A "Blue Ribbon" panel was appointed to study the issues and make recommendations to the council. This they did, and their findings were presented. But the panel went one step further and recommended the council adopt a second ordinance that gave special status under the Human Rights Ordinance to homosexuals. The council approved both these new ordinances on a split vote and ordered their implementation.

A citizens group strongly objected to the ordinances, especially the one giving protection in housing and employment to gays and lesbians, and organized a petition campaign to bring the matter to a vote of the people. Fort Collins businessman, Greg Snyder, led the movement. He was successful in getting enough signatures on petitions to force the council to put the ordinances on the ballot for the next election. A huge public debate ensued. There were even incidents during the campaign. Jim Ringenberg, a Fort Collins lawyer who worked for the opposition to the ordinances reported threatening phone calls, eggs thrown at his house, and his mailbox knocked down. The ordinances came up for vote during the general election in November 1998. The people turned back both ordinances by a two to one majority. Bad feelings resulted from the election. A number of people had grown suspicious of some members of the city council since they felt they should have been better in tune with the feelings of the Fort Collins majority.

Meanwhile more trouble was brewing over another growth issue. Denver developer Mark Goldberg asked for approval to build a new Wal-Mart Superstore and other commercial buildings at the intersection of Mulberry and Lemay. He worked for months with the city staff in satisfying all their objections to building the center. The city was concerned about traffic, the floodplain, the site plan, the size of the building, and many other details. Finally, Goldberg was able to meet all of the city requirements under the published regulations of both the LDGS and the new City Plan. The staff recommended approval to the Planning and Zoning Board. The P&Z Board voted to disapprove the development. Goldberg countered that he had met every requirement and satisfied every regulation. The P&Z board, on a split vote, determined that the data the city used to recommend approval was wrong.

Goldberg appealed the decision to the city council. On a 4 to 3 vote, the council upheld the actions of the P&Z board. Goldberg threatened to sue, or at least, to gather enough signatures on petitions to put this matter on the next election ballot. He was successful in gaining enough signatures, and in the city election on April 6, 1999, the voters overwhelmingly overturned the actions of both the city council and the P&Z board.

DIGGING IN. *Early construction on the new Wal-Mart Supercenter. The entire site was raised several feet to get it out of the floodplain. (Courtesy of Style Magazine)*

In the same election, the city brought forth a plan to dramatically increase the level of public transportation through the Transfort Bus System. The plan also called for the modernization of the traffic light

THEIR HONORS. *Mayors of Fort Collins in the modern era. Front row from left: Robert Sears, Eugene Frink, Harvey Johnson, Thomas Bennett, and Karl Carson. Back row from left: John Knezovich, Kelly Ohlson, Larry Estrada, William Fead, Jack Russell, Earl Wilkinson, Richard Suinn, Chuck Bowling, Barbara Rutstein, Gerry Horak. (Courtesy of Kelly Ohlson)*

system that had not been updated in many years. The computers in most new cars were more sophisticated than the computer that ran the entire traffic light system in Fort Collins. The price tag on that part of the proposal was about $4 million, but the cost of the augmented bus system was almost $90 million. The city planned to pay for the project with an increase of .36% in the sales tax. The voters liked the idea of getting the traffic lights fixed, but they were not willing to pay the big price for the public transportation to get it. The ordinance was defeated three to one.

This misreading of the public by the city council eroded their support. It made any council's job a lot more difficult to do, because now everything they did and every action they took was more closely examined and criticized. For the previous decade, the city council had been the champion of the people in their changing attitudes that demanded input on public policy. The council was, very much, an expression of their will. The people grew to feel that this connection had been lost.

In the fall of 1999, a new issue surfaced. The long debated, but never built, truck bypass was again a topic of discussion. Over the years, the numbers of trucks rolling through Fort Collins from I-25 to Highway 287 increased. The truckers said they took this route because it saved 40 miles rather than going all the way to Cheyenne and joining I-80. Fort Collins citizens didn't like the truck traffic, thought it was dangerous, hard on the streets, and destructive to the downtown historic buildings along Jefferson Street.

The disagreement came over where the bypass should be built. The city staff wanted to use Vine Drive, plus some open land to cut a diagonal that would move the trucks about a mile further north. The residents of the three historic communities of Buckingham, Alta Vista, and Andersonville, vehemently objected to that option. In the first place, the residents didn't want the trucks running through their neighborhood. In the second place, they argued that moving the route only one mile to the north would only put off the problem for a few years until growth had again hemmed in the truck route. The residents thought that an alternate route much further north, would be a better choice.

The city council didn't agree, so the residents of the three neighborhoods began another petition process to bring the matter to a vote of the people. When they had gained enough signatures, the issue went on the November general election ballot, where the voters supported it, and required the city to find another route that was outside of the Urban Growth Boundary of Fort Collins.

On that sour note, the political decade came to a close.

*OPENED IN 1995, the Senior Center serves more than just the senior public. A facility is used by people of all ages. (Courtesy Style Magazine)*

# A Wonderful Senior Center

The publication *Retirement Places Rated*, a national review of all the best places in the country in which to retire is updated every few years. In 1999, Fort Collins was selected as the top place in America to retire. The analysis was based on climate, education, recreation, employment, crime, and housing. Fort Collins finished high enough in each of these categories to earn the Number One rating.

In a radio interview with the author of the book, David Savageau, was asked whether the Fort Collins Senior Center was a factor in the city's selection. He said it wasn't, and that, in fact, he didn't even know the city had a Senior Center.

This amazing revelation came as a great surprise to the officials at the Senior Center. They viewed the facility, opened in 1995, as the best Senior Center in the country. It has 40,000 square foot, multi-use facility. It features a gymnasium, elevated jogging track, lap pool and spa, a stage, a library, pool and snooker room, and a craft studio.

The Senior Center is mobbed with people on a daily basis. Officials estimate that a 1,000 people a day use the building for something. There are literally hundreds of activities, of all kinds, that are offered by the Senior Center. It operates a full schedule of trips. There are day trips, skiing trips, cruises, concerts, bus tours to the gambling towns of Blackhawk and Central City, historical trips, and visits to the Denver

*FIRST-RATE FACILITY. More than 40,000 square feet, the Senior Center serves at least 1,000 people everyday. It offers a myriad of programs. (Courtesy Style Magazine)*

Zoo and Museum.  The list is endless.

On a regular basis, groups from all over the country visit the Fort Collins Senior Center to learn and to model their programs on its success.  The staff at the center is very proud of what they have achieved.  The Senior Center was built with Choices 95 sales tax funding, and was one of the proudest achievements of Mayor Ann Azari, during her three terms as the city's top elected official.

# There's a Lot Right about Fort Collins

In any historical review of the events over a long period of time for a city, there will be high points and low points.  The issues and the major

*LINKAGE. Golfers enjoy one of three public golf courses in Fort Collins. They include City Park nine, Collindale, and Southridge. (Courtesy Style Magazine)*

*EASY TO USE. Fishing in the Fort Collins natural areas is popular and very accommodating. There are many such spots sprinkled throughout the city. (Courtesy Style Magazine)*

events have always been dominant in the chronicle. Sometimes it looks as though the problems have been so all encompassing that it's easy to lose the magic that exists in a city like Fort Collins.

But the list of amenities for this community is very long. There are over 40 parks with well-trimmed lawns and magnificent trees. The parks are equipped with numerous tennis basketball, volleyball, and horseshoe courts, sports fields, playgrounds, picnic facilities, and fishing areas. Golfers may choose from one nine-hole and two 18-hole championship city-owned courses. There are four swimming pools, an archery range, bicycle motocross, outdoor fitness courses, and disc golf course. There are 21 miles in the recreational trail system and 5,000 acres of preserved open space. At City Park you can swim, take a paddle boat ride, fish, or ride the miniature train. The farm at Lee Martinez Park features farm buildings, and animals. You can ride a pony, and the list continues to expand yearly.

A wonderful performing arts center is used almost every day of the year. Major stars appear in the performance hall, and the Fort Collins Symphony Orchestra has delighted audiences for over 50 years.

The EPIC ice center trains hundreds of figure skaters and there are a hundred hockey teams. The figure skating program at EPIC is so advanced that some of the skaters could make most country's Olympic teams.

*WORLD-CLASS. The ice skating program at the EPIC center is one of the very best in the country. Skaters trained here are always among the top finishers in competitions. (Courtesy Style Magazine)*

The streets are wide, the crime rates low, the educational facilities at both the Poudre School District, and Colorado State University are first rate.

These things didn't just happen. The people of Fort Collins have made them happen through planning, hard work, and imagination over the past half century. From a small town with a lot of potential and less than 15,000 in 1950, to a sophisticated city of 112,000 at the turn of the century, Fort Collins has more to be proud of then any other city in the world. The people of Fort Collins invest in the future, are proud of their diversity, fight like lions, and pull together when the times get rough.

Fort Collins is more than just a town; It's a state of mind. How it handles defeat is at least as important as how it handles victory. One of the of the most amazing things about the people making up this community is that they have always believed that no challenge is too great to face, no adversity too large to bear, no opportunity too small to let pass. This is a rare commodity. It is strength, that Fort Collins is going to need, a lot, in the next 100 years.

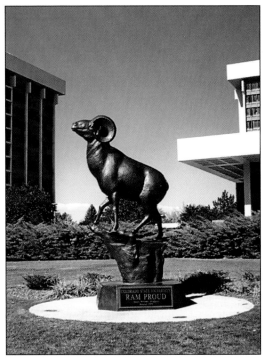

*RAM PROUD. It says so on the base of the statue, and could be said for all the people who live in Fort Collins. (Courtesy Style Magazine)*

# Into the Future

In the January 2nd edition of the Fort Collins Express Courier, in 1896, Fort Collins Mayor Fred Baker was asked to give his predictions of what the city would be like 100 years in the future. His predictions had an amazing reality to them as we reflect on his foresight.

Baker said that in 1996 Fort Collins would have a population of 100,000. At the time he wrote this, the city had a population of 3,000. How he could have gotten the number so accurate is amazing. He said the 90% of the people would be engaged in the manufacturing of batteries, buttons, wires, and wheels. Baker predicted that homes would be on pivots that could be rotated to suit the whims of the owner to take advantage of weather or scenery. He said that these homes would be heated in the winter and cooled in the summer by electricity.

This mayor predicted that women would have pockets in their clothing. He was equally certain that there would be little difference between the way men and women dressed. Baker believed that no man or woman would be allowed to vote unless they understood electrical engineering.

In commerce, Baker saw the end of the steam railroad. He thought stores would be open all night, and that delivery from stores would come as packages that were sent through tubes, powered by electricity.

Perhaps the most interesting of all his predictions was his idea that people would be able to sit at their desk and communicate directly with someone in New York or San Francisco by pushing a button. He said that this communication would come in writing to people everywhere.

No doubt, the people of Fort Collins in 1896 got quite a chuckle out of these fanciful predictions. However, today the people of Fort Collins can only shake their heads that Fred Baker had so much of it right.

What about the next hundred years? What kind of predictions would come to mind for a Fort Collins in the year 2100?

Baker was a product of his time and he was projecting hopes and dreams as much as he was predicting the future. Much the same could probably be said for the people of today. When the citizens of this community look forward to the years to come, it's likely they will want to see solutions for the problems they experience today. The wish list for Fort Collins would be answers to traffic, sprawl, growth, the environment, and quality of life.

Clearly, the next 100 years will bring an end of dependence on fossil fuels. The petroleum supply will be gone long before a century has passed. However, the near future will certainly bring the opening of the hydrogen economy. The implications of that are monumental. The hydrogen economy will mean that it will no longer be necessary for individual homes, or businesses to be connected to a central power grid. Power will be generated inside of each building. Part of the reason for living in cities is because of the availability of the energy sources.

The by-product of using hydrogen as a fuel source is water. Just as water was the lifeblood for the people of northern Colorado throughout its history, an independently produced source of water will mean an even greater emancipation for them.

The hydrogen economy will not produce pollutants. None of the engines that power society today will release any pollution if the energy source is hydrogen. In a hundred years, the air will be much cleaner and healthier.

Overlaying a totally new energy source are the existing and rapidly emerging computer systems. E-commerce has already become a major way of life. This trend is not going to diminish, but rather will intensify.

Much more sophisticated computers are on the near horizon. In a hundred years, humanity will have long become accustomed to simply talking to their computers and receiving whatever information they wish, or buying and selling whatever they need. Communications will be global, instantaneous, visible on screens, and interactive.

These certain developments will surely create a living environment that is far less dependent on compacted city living. Products could be produced in automated facilities and delivered mechanically by robotic machines. The service industry could be no further away then around

COMMUNITY EVENTS. Riverfest has been one of the most popular of the city festivals. It celebrates the Poudre River. (Courtesy Style Magazine)

the corner in your home. Business and schools could be in offices and classrooms where you live. It would not matter where you lived, only how you lived.

Does this mean that city living is likely to become a thing of the past? Probably not. People don't live in cities just for convenience and economics. They chose to live together because man is a social animal, gregarious and interactive. Most people would not choose to live in a far corner of a forest with no contact with other people. Rather they would choose to enjoy the company of others and the stimulation it provides. A successful city of the future would know that entertainment, recreation, continuing education, the arts, and social opportunities of every kind, would be the keys to maintaining a viable community. These are the components of quality of life today,

*AWAY FROM IT AL, and close to where people live, the 21 miles of bike trails in Fort Collins are a popular way to exercise and relax. (Courtesy Style Magazine)*

and would be even more so in the future.

What clues does this give us to building a Fort Collins of the future? It means that the city and its citizens should reach out in every way to embrace each element of new technology that is available. It should seek out ways to incorporate these new tools into our daily lives in the shortest time possible. Fort Collins needs to have the vision to forecast our short term and long term future and plan for it. The total population will need to lift its eyes beyond the immediate band-aid solutions to problems that has driven public policy for too long, and see more meaningful and rewarding long-term goals.

As the city moves into a more sophisticated and advanced posture, it needs to take up the results of these improvements and begin to

*A NEW DAWN is coming to Fort Collins. The people welcome it and are eager for all that the new day offers. (Courtesy of John Clarke)*

concentrate on the quality of life it will produce. This means that diversions, amenities and special features that have been considered luxuries till now, will become the imperatives of the future.

If Fort Collins is successful is driving technology to produce quality of life, then the environment will improve, traffic will shift to efficient, affordable public transportation that people will actually use, and there will be wonderful new places for the community to see, embrace and enjoy. Moreover, it will not matter that there will be a quarter of a million people living in Fort Collins 25 years from now.

Almost a hundred years ago, historian Ansel Watrous wrote of the people of Fort Collins, *"All those who came here in the early days were men with strong, vigorous constitutions, level-headed, brave of heart, energetic and enterprising, and filled with a desire to plant the banner of civilization in the wilderness."*

A hundred years from now, the same should be said of today's residents of this city, as the newest crop of pioneers out here on the wild frontier, summon the future and build a new future Vision Along the Poudre Valley.

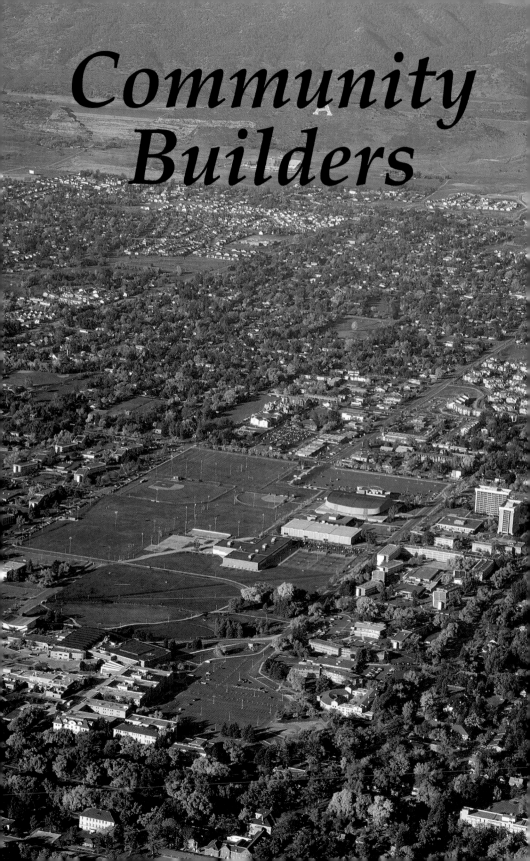

# Community Builders

# Community Builders

## THE HARMONY CORRIDOR
### Golden Entrance to Fort Collins

As the city of Fort Collins grew to the south, Harmony Road began to grow in importance. This was emphasized in the 1970s when a huge new employer came to town. Hewlett-Packard made the decision to place a major center in Fort Collins and they chose to locate on Harmony Road. HP was destined to become the second largest employer in Fort Collins, behind Colorado State University, and would grow to 3,500 employees by the year 2,000. A number of other enterprises spun off of HP as well. Celestica and Agilent were both outcomes of the HP

*A new shopping area has developed at the corner of College and Harmony.*

presence in Fort Collins. Additionally, a number of smaller high-tech companies were formed independently or from former employees of HP. The economic impact of HP on the city is enormous.

By the beginning of the 1990s, it was obvious that a comprehensive plan for the Harmony Corridor was needed. Working toward this end, Bob Everitt contacted all the property owners on Harmony and asked them to get together for a meeting to make a plan for the corridor. Everitt believed that an attractive entrance to the city was needed, and also that the corridor should become a major employment center.

Present at the initial meeting were; The Everitt Companies, Hewlett-Packard, GT Land, who owned the property at the corner of Harmony and Lemay, Bill Tiley, Calvin and Glen Johnson, Elmer Stromberger, and others who had an interest on Harmony. The group met and agreed that a plan should be prepared. They also agreed that the City of Fort Collins should be included in the planning as well. Tom Peterson, who was the city planner at that time, was contacted.

The City was very interested. They wanted a coordinated plan, not a hodgepodge. They also wanted to insure that development on the corridor itself was confined to commercial and industrial concerns, and that residential building should be placed behind the business centers. The City appointed a committee to study the corridor and to make recommendations to the city council on how it should be developed. The process took a year and a half.

A final draft of the corridor plan, including roads, traffic signal coordination, landscaping, bike paths, and greenbelts was prepared. It included

*Hewlett-Packard is the second largest employer in Fort Collins.*

the entire corridor from College Avenue to I-25 and a half-mile back on both sides of Harmony road. The plan was submitted to the city council in 1993 and approved.

Since that time, the Harmony Corridor has developed steadily. The Pioneer Mobile Home Park at the corner of College and Harmony was redeveloped into commercial shopping. The strip from Boardwalk to Lemay was developed for restaurants, a Steele's Market, Sam's Club, and Builders Square. Celestica and LSI Logic both built on the corridor. A major movie theater, Cinemark, was built at the corner of Timberline and Lemay, and Poudre Valley Hospital opened its Harmony campus in the fall of 2000. Plus other commercial operations have also been built, including the new Group Real Estate building, A Courtyard and Residence Inn by Marriot, several other hotels, restaurants, and commercial office buildings.

The Harmony Corridor is now the most important employment center in Fort Collins with as many as 10,000 jobs along its route. Bob Everitt believes that the corridor is the most important commercial addition to Fort Collins in its history and is confident that it will become even more so in the future.

191

# STRYKER SHORT FOUNDATION
## *Committed To Building Community*

The Stryker Short Foundation was established in 1995 by Pat and Tommy Short. It is Larimer County's largest private foundation. The Foundation targets grants in three principal areas, mostly in Larimer County. The emphasis is on youth, the environment, and the arts.

*Pat Short*

Pat Short, President of the Foundation, says, "We've been blessed. We love Fort Collins and northern Colorado. Through the Foundation, we hope to help our community achieve its goals and dreams." Pat grew up in Michigan, the middle of three children and granddaughter of Dr. Homer Hartman Stryker, founder of Stryker Corporation, a world-renowned manufacturer of specialty medical equipment. Pat moved to Fort Collins in 1980 after attending the University of Northern Colorado.

Pat is actively involved in the community, generously devoting time and energy to running the Stryker Short Foundation, volunteering at Harris Elementary School, serving as President of the Harmony Reservoir Recreation Association, sitting on the Colorado State University Development Council, and serving as a board member for the Center for Community Justice Partnerships.

Tommy Short is Chairman of Bohemian Companies and Vice President of the Stryker Short Foundation. He is a global entrepreneur and philanthropist who believes building successful communities starts at home. He says, "Hard work, honesty, integrity, and building solid relationships are the keys to a strong family, a thriving community, and an enduring environment."

Tommy moved to Colorado in 1979 after attending the University of Oregon, where he studied political science.

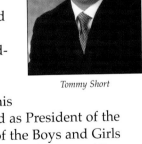
*Tommy Short*

Tommy's extensive civic involvement models his belief in the rewards of hard work. He has served as President of the Downtown Business Association, and President of the Boys and Girls Club of Larimer County. Currently he is a member of the City of Fort Collins' Lincoln Center, Board of Directors, and the Fort Collins Area Chamber of Commerce.

Youth involvement is a major outreach of the Foundation. The

Stryker Short Foundation strongly believes tomorrow's dynamic community can become real if children and young adults are supported and enriched today. Through thoughtful programs that impact wide populations and inspire individuals committed to youth, this goal is being achieved. In 2000, Stryker Short Foundation gave $2 million to the Boys and Girls Club for a new facility and for an endowment to personnel.

Other youth programs supported by the Foundation include, The Poudre School District, Project Self-Sufficiency, Learning is Fun Field Trip Fund, Bilingual Elementary Learning, Namaqua Center, Colorado State University, and the Fort Collins Soccer Club.

The environment is of special concern to the Stryker Short Foundation. To consolidate operating costs and provide one-of-a-kind service, Colorado State University, Colorado State Parks, the City of Fort Collins, and Colorado Department of Public Affairs agreed to create the state's only Welcome Center that offers extensive educational opportunities and outdoor learning. The Stryker

*Committed to youth and the environment, Stryker Short Foundation finds ways to help.*

Short Foundation awarded $325,000 to fund development of the Environmental Learning Center, which opened outside of Fort Collins in spring 2000. The Center features a 5-acre site that includes an outdoor amphitheater, children's exploration walk, connecting to the current Environmental Learning Center, and numerous natural areas. Ranger talks, a youth ranger corps, community events and opportunities for students to learn environmental education are also available.

Continuing support is given to the Larimer Land Trust, Nature Conservancy, the Phantom Canyon Open Space purchase, Devil's Backbone, and Rocky Mountain National Park.

The final anchor of the Stryker Short Foundation's support emphasis is for the Arts. "Music is a language we all share: it communicates to all ages," says Tommy Short. The Foundation provides approximately $100,000 per year to underwrite the musical portion of NewWestFest, an annual three-day event. The free concerts offer all Fort Collins residents, especially families and youth, the opportunity to hear and see some of today's best popular talent. The concerts attract more than 15,000 people per year.

In 2000, The Stryker Short Foundation gave a $1 million grant to the CSU Center for the Arts. They also support the Open Stage Theater, Fort Collins Symphony, and the Serendipity Youth Arts Program.

# WHEELER PROPERTIES
## *Development with A purpose*

From 1972 through 1976, Bill Neal was the Planning Director for the City of Greeley. When he left that job, he became associated with prominent Greeley builder and developer, John R.P. Wheeler. In 1981, Neal moved to Fort Collins to oversee the Wheeler building projects at The Brown Farm. That subdivision was built on 440 acres of land in west Fort Collins and had 1,100 homes in it.

By 1982, Neal was busy with Drake Crossing Shopping Center at the corner of Drake and Shields. The anchors for the center were Safeway and Walgreen's. It was designed to be the commercial support center

*Poudre Valley Plaza at the corner of Horsetooth and Shields is designed in Western Territorial style.*

for all the homes that had been built in The Brown Farm.

The Fairbrooke subdivision was begun in 1986, Neal planned and built 350 housing units on 90 acres. These homes were medium priced for a wide range of buyers.

Despite a cloudy economic picture, Neal went ahead with two new commercial centers in the mid 1980s. These were Cimarron Square and Raintree Village Shopping Centers. By the end of the 1980s, both centers had experienced difficult economic times. Nevertheless, Neal continued to market the centers and they have both recovered today.

In 1997, Neal set out to build his multiple-use, commercial, retail and residential center at Poudre Valley Plaza, he had more in mind than just another development at the corner of two busy Fort Collins streets. What he wanted was a center with the character, integrity and historical faithfulness that was would reflect the lifestyle of our community.

194

Poudre Valley Plaza blends the best architectural styles that have become famous in Colorado history. The overall theme is called Colorado Western Territorial. It encompasses native sandstone cut from the same quarries that built CSU. It uses structural steel similar to steel buildings built in Colorado from the Civil War to the turn of the century. The roof tiles are the same that came from the old, downtown Fort Collins post office that was built in 1903. The result is a distinctive and beautiful center that stands out from all the rest.

The most recent project of Wheeler Properties and Bill Neal is the 310-acre Rigden Farm in southeast Fort Collins. It was the first major subdivision that was built under the new City Plan guidelines. Rigden Farm promotes containing urban sprawl through higher densities and mixed-use areas, but Neal says people will not be forced to live on smaller lots.

Rigden Farm is dedicated to a philosophy of creating a community and not just a housing development. It will be a fully integrated

*The statue of Antoine Janis, the Poudre Valley's first white settler, stands proudly on the corner.*

neighborhood with a diverse array of housing from high end to affordable town homes. It will also feature a church, grocery store, town square, and an internal transportation (trail) system. For a look that is

reminiscent of the turn of the century, there will be apartments located above commercial buildings in a pedestrian shopping area.

Another dream project for Neal is the redevelopment of the downtown urban river corridor. This is primarily the land along the river, downtown, from College Avenue to the Lincoln Street Bridge. There are dozens of property owners in the area, including the biggest property owner of them all, the City of Fort Collins. But Neal is optimistic that he can bring all the parties together and redevelop the river corridor in such a way that it will respect the environment of the river, while still providing a pleasant place for people to shop, and seek out recreation and entertainment.

*Bill Neal*

Bill Neal continues to find new ways to build for Fort Collins in a way that contributes to better lifestyles and a sense of community. He believes that building isn't all about brick and mortar. It's also about the sensitivity to six generations of people who made our city what it is today.

# SITZMAN-MITCHELL COMPANY
## *Continuing the Dream*

The list of achievements in Fort Collins development for Gene
Mitchell and his company is long and distinguished. Beginning in the
1970s with Scotch Pines, Scotch Pines Village Shopping Center, at the

*The Marriott sits in the center of the Arena District with other Sitzman-Mitchell properties nearby.*

corner of Drake and Lemay, The Square shopping Center in 1978, and
the development of the Arena property.

In the 1980s, Mitchell turned his attention to downtown and his
dream of rebuilding the original blocks of Fort Collins. This resulted in
the construction of Old Town Square in 1983. At the same time, the Fort
Collins Marriott was built near the corner of Horsetooth and College. It
was a $16 million project that was completed in 1985.

The turbulence of the financial markets in the late 1980s brought the
Mitchell Company to the brink of disaster. Mitchell was forced to give
up most of his properties in a series of restructuring moves that shrunk
the company from over 40 to under 10 people.

By 1989, Mitchell had turned most of the day to day operations of the
company over to young Dave Sitzman, who systematically worked one
problem at a time and started the company back to a more profitable

picture. The company was renamed Sitzman-Mitchell Company.

From 1990 to 1996, using the model he had learned from Gene Mitchell, which was to build for quality, and try to always make a statement that improved the community, Sitzman began expansion of his own. He built a new building next to the Marriott, and helped to develop several others. The improving financial picture

*Gene Mitchell*

allowed the company to reacquire many of the properties lost in the 1980s. Scotch Pines Village remains a part of the company, as does the Wells Fargo Bank building. A favorable partnership with the Everitt Companies allowed for the final disposition of the Marriott Hotel and the development of the Courtyard and Residence Inn of the Marriott Corporation on the Harmony Corridor.

*Dave Sitzman*

In 1996, Sitzman-Mitchell embarked on a completely new project in Berthoud. The company developed Berthoud Village. This development was sensitive to the character of that community and gave it an identity that fit into the history of Berthoud. It was a part of the town, instead of being just a commercial addition. It has been successful from the beginning.

Gene Mitchell is not shy about giving credit and applause to his protégé who has combined good business principals with charm and grace in building. He believes that if it had not been for Dave Sitzman, that, in his words, "I would have been toast a long time ago."

# FIRST NATIONAL BANK
## *A Solid Sign of Community Success*

"In reflecting on Fort Collins and the reasons why we are so enamoured by our lifestyle, we can quote the obvious: wide streets and open minds for growth; climate and proximity to mountains; and above all, the wonderful feeling we have for the community. From my perspective, it's the people in our community and their pride in Fort Collins that makes it so choice."

*Tom Gleason, Chairman of the Board.*

"As we know, it didn't just happen. It started with such visionary pioneers as the Masons, Stovers, Hottels, and scores of others over some 140 years. We have been blessed with outstanding leadership in the public sector as well as the private sector. They have all been dedicated to preserving, protecting, and enhancing the culture and lifestyle of Fort Collins." Tom Gleason, Chairman of the Board.

The First National Bank is the largest banking institution in Fort Collins and northern Colorado. It has an asset base of more than $900 million. In 1991, the bank was categorized fourth best in earnings for the state of Colorado. It is one of the major employers in the city of Fort Collins with over 300 employees.

The bank was established in 1880 as the Larimer County Bank. It changed its name to First National Bank the following year. It became a federally chartered bank in 1934 under the name First National Bank and has provided full banking services since that time.

From 1956 until 1991, the bank was a part of the Western Bancorporation of Los Angeles and evolved into what was known as First Interstate Bank. This relationship ended in 1991 and the bank became an independent operation under the newly created holding company, Larimer Bancorporation.

In October 1993, the bank became affiliated with the First National of Nebraska. The following year, the bank changed its name back to First National Bank, with the slogan, "We're Still First." The association with the First National Bank of Omaha continues until today. The newly formed holding company, of which First National is a part, is a $7 billion

*The First National Bank building and tower.*

company with over 4,000 employees.

The First National continues to expand. It has added five new locations since 1996. These locations include the Loveland Trust office, Loveland Main office, North College office, Southwest office, and the newest at Colorado State University. Along with the full-service branch at 155 Boardwalk, the bank is proud of its growth.

From its humble beginning in 1880, to the challenge of the millennium, First National Bank is committed to growth and prosperity by offering ~ Quality Products and Superior Service.

# W.W. REYNOLDS COMPANIES
## *Building to Last*

Boulder native Bill Reynolds has been creating practical, comfortable, and professional office space in Boulder and Fort Collins for over a quarter of a century.

*Prospect East is a pleasant setting for the office buildings designed by The W.W. Reynolds Companies.*

Reynolds is the visionary president and founder of The W.W. Reynolds Companies.

His heritage of growing up in Boulder has given him a unique perspective in the design of office buildings. In fact, his idea of making an office center a pleasant atmosphere was revolutionary when he began the process in the 1970s with his development of the Table Mesa Shopping Center.

Reynolds was soon expanding out of Boulder and into Fort Collins. He built his first building at 2716 S. College in 1973. He still owns the building, believing that you build to last and hold on to what you have.

Other enterprises followed. In the 1980s, a couple of fellows with a big idea came to Reynolds and told him that the office space they were renting from him on Lincoln Avenue was not large enough. Reynolds wanted to know about how much space they thought they would need. The answer was an enormous 26,000 square foot building. After considerable arm-twisting and grand planning, the two men convinced

Reynolds, and the bank, that their idea was indeed worth the risk.

That's how Doug Schatz and Brent Bachman got the space to expand their new company called Advanced Energy.

Reynolds acquired 90 acres of land on Prospect Street, east of Timberline Road. At that time, this land was on the extreme fringe of development for Fort Collins. Nevertheless, the land had everything that was important to Reynolds. It was close to the Poudre River, there was open land around it. It was quiet and scenic. Reynolds designed a new kind of office center. He built a pond, and a park. He made sure there was good circulation for traffic. He didn't do this just for the aesthetics; there was a practical thought in his mind. If you build an attractive atmosphere for your office buildings, you will also build value. You will also create a space that people will want to rent and use.

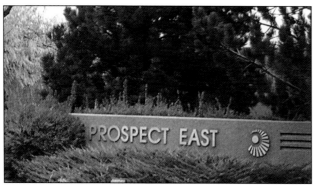
*A unique setting builds value.*

As Reynolds puts it, "We try to build things that our clients will appreciate and be willing to pay for. We want to have a nice feel for our areas, not monuments to the builders ego."

It's a model that has worked for many years. Reynolds' designed office space has an eye to the future needs of a business. He believes that clean, simple spaces respond more easily to the changing face of business than to trendy experimental designs that can become dated and unusable in a very short time. All of Reynolds' buildings offer well-lit spaces, plenty of windows, a pleasant view, and an understated professional atmosphere. Comfort and function, not elegance, are the trademarks of Reynolds buildings.

Reynolds is an avid outdoorsman and loves the natural world. He brings as much of that to his office parks as he can. He reasons that people like to work in places that are close to bike paths, rivers, ponds, and plenty of green grass. His Prospect East is a perfect example of that principal put into action.

The W.W. Reynolds Companies, the Boulder companies that came to Fort Collins and made it better.

# THE CHARCO-BROILER
## *Standing the Test of Time*

When Gib McGarvey looks at his restaurant, The Charco-Broiler, he doesn't see a building, he sees people. He sees the people who cook the food, serve the food, and eat the food. He knows that if the food

*The Charco-Broiler makes Christmas fun for its employees.*

is of superior quality, and if the people, are all treated right, then he has nothing else to worry about. It's a formula that has worked perfectly since 1957.

In a world of fast food, corporate portion controls, and bottom line management, the Charco-Broiler does not fit the mold at all. It is a splendid anachronism that has been successful for so long, it's become an institution.

The fact of the matter is that many of the people who work at the Charco-Broiler have been there for decades. An employee with less than ten years of service is considered a newcomer. This is unheard of in an era when lengthy service at a restaurant is often measured in weeks.

Why does the Charco-Broiler have such a record of success? Obviously, Gib McGarvey takes care of his employees. He has a simple philosophy. If you take care of your people, trust them, treat them with respect and loyalty, you will receive the same from them.

202

This translates into a homey, folksy, atmosphere. People love to eat at the Charco-Broiler. There is real reliability in going there. When you add the certain promise of getting the best quality food, you have all the ingredients for a forever formula.

*Gib and Lynn McGarvey*

McGarvey is also a community builder. It was his idea that prodded a reluctant radio broadcaster into starting a series of radio programs telling about the history of Fort Collins. The broadcaster was certain nobody would be interested. He was wrong. McGarvey has a sense of what the public wants and enjoys. After a while, the entire "Visions Along the Poudre Valley" series had developed a life of its own. That life continues even till today when 569 original radio programs, 8 hour-long audiocassettes, a video, a calendar, and two books have been produced from a single idea by one, very good man.

A "Visions" production could not go forth without including the Charco-Broiler in the mix. Its as much a part of us, as he is of Fort Collins.

# COLDWELL BANKER
## EVERITT & WILLIAMS REAL ESTATE
### *A Real Estate Leader*

As Northern Colorado continues to grow and flourish Coldwell Banker Everitt & Williams Real Estate has been an industry leader every step of the way for the past 31 years.

In the late 1960's, Founder/Partner Bob Everitt owned a lumberyard on North College, which is now the site of the Old Town Car Wash. The

*The new offices of Coldwell Banker on Drake Street*

Fort Collins' real estate market at the time was going through a rather dismal period and local builders were having a difficult time finding lots to build homes. Naturally, Mr. Everitt became equally concerned for his lumberyard and took it upon himself to support the real estate community as a whole. He borrowed some money from his father in order to purchase and develop plots of land. Thus, Everitt Realty was founded in 1969.

Gus Williams, President/Partner joined Coldwell Banker Everitt Real Estate in 1984 and partnered with the Everitt's in 1988. Now in its 31st year, Coldwell Banker Everitt & Williams is the largest full service real estate and relocation company in northern Colorado. Today, Coldwell Banker Everitt & Williams continues to pride itself on what every customer expects from a real estate firm when making the largest decision of their life: knowledge, service and integrity. It is their philosophy that each customer and each transaction made is

*Gus Williams, President*

treated with these company values.

Coldwell Banker Everitt & Williams Real Estate is in the business of bringing buyers and sellers of real estate together-creating opportunities for them to achieve their objectives and shepherding transactions which result in desired benefits to both. The mission of the company is to continually improve their professional abilities and to meet the needs of their clients and customers with accurate information, prudent advice, and expeditious action.

Coldwell Banker Everitt & Williams has four convenient offices with 165 full-time associates. They are the primary real estate company in Fort Collins, Windsor and Greeley representing the largest relocation company in the world, Cendant Mobility! They are proud to be the Premier Real Estate and Relocation Company in Northern Colorado.